THE NEW
enlightened

SIMPLE RECIPES FOR EXTRAORDINARY LIVING

CAROLINE MARIE DUPONT

books
Alive

Summertown, Tennessee

Library of Congress Cataloging-in-Publication Data

Dupont, Caroline Marie.
    The new enlightened eating : simple recipes for extraordinary living / Caroline Marie Dupont.
       p. cm.
    Includes index.
    ISBN 978-0-920470-83-1 (pbk.) — ISBN 978-1-57067-940-7 (e-book)
  1. Cooking (Natural foods)   2. Vegan cooking.   3. Health.   I. Title.
    TX741.D8524 2012
    641.5'636—dc23

2012004055

Front cover: Cilantro Tempeh, p. 166
Back cover (from top): Harvest Fruit Salad, p. 42, Orange-Oatmeal Muffins, p. 50,
Sweet Curried Rice and Vegetables, p. 144, Chocolate Mousse Pie, p. 172

Cover and interior design: John Wincek
Cover and interior photos: Warren Jefferson
Food styling: Barbara Jefferson, Ron Maxen

Printed on recycled paper

Book Publishing Co. is a member of Green Press Initiative. We chose to print this title on paper with postconsumer recycled content, processed without chlorine, which saved the following natural resources:

88 trees
2,550 pounds of solid waste
40, 221 gallons of wastewater
8, 919 pounds of greenhouse gases
36 million BTU of total energy

For more information, visit greenpressinitiative.org.

Paper calculations from Environmental Defense Paper Calculator, edf.org/papercalculator.

© 2012 Caroline Marie Dupont

Books Alive
a division of Book Publishing Company
415 Farm Road
P.O. Box 99
Summertown, TN 38483
888-260-8458
bookpubco.com

ISBN 13: 978-0-920470-83-1

18 17 16 15 14 13 12   1 2 3 4 5 6 7 8 9

CONTENTS

To my children, Jérémie and Jacqueline, and to the child in each one of us who naturally lives guided by the heart.

May you create your most blessed life

moment to moment

by profoundly connecting to your true nature,

questioning limiting thoughts and beliefs,

letting go of emotions that no longer serve you,

and caring for the body, which houses your sacred human experience.

May you recognize the potential for all challenges

to be a doorway into the unparalleled joy of self-discovery.

May you know the depths of your heart.

FOREWORD

There has been a tremendous change in people's attitudes toward food and nutrition in the past ten years. Expert advice is available everywhere: through magazine articles, books, the Internet, and every other means of communication. The average consumer is well on his or her way to becoming better educated and more knowledgeable about what to eat. Even corporate owners of fast-food chains have begun to recognize the need to include healthful food choices on their menus in order to hang on to their market, making it easy to see that progress is occurring.

This progress can be credited to growing global awareness regarding the role of nutrition in our lives and health. This awareness, however, is only the tip of the iceberg. The realization of the importance of diet and its affect on human health can (and should) inspire personal responsibility and a better understanding of the interconnection of body, mind, and spirit. In other words, feeding the body properly feeds the mind and soul as well.

Most of us are still relatively new to this advanced concept of nutrition. Some, by the gift of an uncommon wisdom, have already made giant steps in that direction. The author of this book, Caroline Marie Dupont, is one of those gifted people. She not only understands intimately the relationship between what we eat and who we are, but also applies this knowledge to her own life and shares it generously with all who will listen.

I believe that in the next decade we will see a strong movement toward improving the quality and safety of our food supply. This will bring us closer to nature, the great provider. It will direct our attention to our own communities as the ideal source of nourishing, healthful foods. Hopefully we will see a resurgence of interest in gardening, local farming, and organic practices and enterprises.

The way is simple, really, and we can confidently follow Caroline as she leads us toward better health.

Danielle Perrault, RHN
DIRECTOR, CANADIAN SCHOOL OF NATURAL NUTRITION

v

PREFACE

I don't remember exactly when I decided that I would write a book to share my explorations of nutrition, health, and growth of the soul, but it was quite some time ago. Over the years I've taught many classes and workshops and have created handouts to share ideas and recipes. Eventually I accumulated so much written material that it was obvious that a book was in gestation. Among the many options available, it seemed easiest to pursue the self-published route, and many people came my way to help with the first edition of *Enlightened Eating*.

In this revised edition some sections have been completely rewritten to represent my continued learning and deeper perspective. Here are some of the primary changes:

- I've simplified the steps in many recipes without compromising the end result so that you can make delicious food as efficiently as possible.

- I've revised recipes to avoid calling for some hard-to-find or unusual ingredients, allowing you to make the recipes in this book with readily available ingredients or what you have on hand.

- I am more committed than ever to local foods, and that is reflected in the new recipes and some tweaks to the original recipes.

- I've reduced the amount of salt in most of the recipes and eliminated it entirely from some. This reflects my own preference and a growing awareness that using less salt is better. When you do use salt, I recommend gray Celtic or Normandy sea salt or pink Himalayan salt because of the beneficial trace minerals they contain. Note that people with cancer or other conditions related to impaired immunity or weakness in the kidneys should greatly reduce their salt consumption or avoid it altogether.

- I've revised recipes to avoid using certain ingredients, such as Bragg Liquid Aminos and agave syrup (see sidebar), after learning about their not-so-healthful effects.

- Some of the recipes originally called for frying vegetables like onions, leeks, and garlic in oil. However, heating oils dramatically changes the structure of their fatty acids, especially if the oil has significant amounts of polyunsaturated fatty acids, which are very easily damaged by heat. Monounsaturated and saturated fats, which predominate in olive and coconut oil and, to a lesser extent, sesame oil, are more heat-resistant. Therefore, these are the main oils I call for in heated dishes. In addition, I've revised many of the methods so that vegetables begin cooking in a small amount of water, or oil and water, which keeps the oil cooler. For those with cancer or other serious health conditions, it's best to avoid all heated oils.

- Finally, certain sections have been completely removed and will be covered in depth in a future book on deep healing through living foods and spiritual awareness.

I pray that faithful readers and new readers alike will find in these pages inspiration, enjoyment, and awakened potential for a blessed life.

Joy,
Caroline

Who Knew?

Bragg Liquid Aminos contains glutamic acid as a result of the manufacturing process. Although glutamic acid is a naturally occurring amino acid, it's closely related to monosodium glutamate (MSG), and some people experience similar problematic effects from consuming glutamic acid, including me. I suffered from unexplainable muscle twitches for years as a result of this "health" product, but that symptom reversed almost overnight when I eliminated Bragg Liquid Aminos from my diet.

When the original edition of this book came out, agave nectar was touted as the new healthful sweetener. Since then much controversy has arisen over its manufacturing. Apparently most agave is not as raw as the producers claim. There is also concern about potential negative effects on the liver because of its extremely high levels of fructose. While small amounts of agave syrup are probably okay, I've decided to use maple syrup when a liquid sweetener is needed. This is also best from an environmental stance, as agave plants are destroyed in the manufacturing of the syrup, while maple trees can be tapped for many years when treated with care.

ACKNOWLEDGMENTS

My life has been blessed by support from a seemingly unending number of sources. I would like to express my deepest gratitude to some of those who made important contributions to this book in a variety of ways.

My mother, Gisèle, gave me my first experiences in the kitchen and nurtured a deep respect for the act of caring for and honoring people through food. Together, she and my father, John, whose steadfastness and dedication to his family never wavered, create a solid and safe foundation for me to explore an authentic life. I have learned so much from both of my children, Jérémie and Jacqueline. They inspired me from our very first encounters and are shining examples of soulful living and health. Many of these recipes were created because of my desire to nourish them as well as I possibly could.

I am grateful for the ongoing opportunity to teach at the Canadian School of Natural Nutrition. Danielle Perrault had faith in me as a teacher when the school was taking its first steps, Lisa Tsakos helped to pave the way, and Leslie Gould, Vivian Lee, Caroline Steiss, Pat Ward, and all of the instructors continue to give me comfort and company on this path of educating people about the profound importance of eating well. I've also had the pleasure of meeting thousands of open and sincere students who help me learn what I want to embody.

I am deeply thankful to Bob and Cynthia Holzapfel and all the good people at Book Publishing Company for all they have done to usher this book into the world. Jo Stepaniak patiently and firmly guided me through the editing process and made the book much better. Valerie Colwell kindly reviewed this new edition and offered some important suggestions. When I wrote the original edition, Cathy Russell tirelessly encouraged me and made important contributions. Cesan d'Ornellas Levine generously gave her brilliant artwork. The "Enlightened Ladies" formed an impromptu test kitchen by meeting regularly and over time preparing every single recipe in the first edition of *Enlightened Eating*. Wow! You are all amazing and beautiful, and I thank you for your helpful suggestions. Debbie and Barb and the dedicated staff of Health Management Books, in Canada, have enthusiastically distributed *Enlightened Eating* from the beginning.

I feel fortunate to have friends and family who believe in me. I am grateful that Adyashanti has pointed the way with humility, brilliance, and love. And I am blessed to have Dave, who holds my hand, makes me laugh, and shares my life.

INTRODUCTION
The Heart's Way to Health

This book has been written for you. I want to make holistic nutrition and healthful eating accessible to you—and to as many people as possible. I want you to know or remember that enlightened eating can be a friendly, fun, and elegant process. I want to inspire you by sharing the incredible benefits that healthful eating has not only for physical health but also for mental and emotional health and, most importantly, for your connection to your authentic nature.

Enlightened Eating represents my journey into the compelling and powerful world of nutrition over the course of more than twenty years. In these pages you will find gleanings from many food philosophies, including vegetarianism, veganism, macrobiotics, ayurveda, natural hygiene, and raw foods. My hope is that the information it contains will appeal to everyone interested in health, regardless of where they are in their individual journeys.

As a longtime practicing nutritionist, I've found that people generally sense that food choices are one of the most powerful determinants of health and vitality—and yet this is one of the areas where they struggle the most, for a variety of reasons. We face an on-slaught of information about nutrition and health in the media, much of it conflicting. The number of new books on health and nutrition is similarly overwhelming, and again often creates confusion because of the wide variety of opinions and approaches promoted. Many people feel overscheduled and stressed and therefore find it difficult to make time to shop and prepare meals from scratch. Some people find that family members and other loved ones are unwilling to go along with healthful food choices.

In this book I've provided tried-and-true recipes that I've been preparing for my family, friends, and students for many years. In addition, you'll find inspirational and practical information that will guide you toward a greater understanding of your relationship with food, making it easier for you to select and prepare foods that are healthful and healing. I honor the uniqueness of each person's adventure in seeking nutritional excellence. The most successful journey is one that leaves you feeling vibrant and integrates wholeness, health, and peace, while also making the best use of your time and respecting the need to please and nourish family members and loved ones.

A Natural Path to Health and Healing

The path to health is both simple and potentially challenging. On the one hand, the answers to many questions about healthful eating can be found inside each of us. Nature has always provided nutritious foods, and we all have the ability to access the intuition that can guide us to choose the best foods for ourselves and our loved ones. On the other hand, Western society is painfully alienated from the natural world, and many of us are also estranged from an intimate relationship with our bodies and souls. We need to learn to trust our bodies to lead us in health-supporting directions. Often the first step is slowing down and getting still enough to hear and listen to this inner guidance.

It's well-known that fresh, natural, high-quality foods create healthier bodies. Virtually every disorder can be prevented, improved, or healed through food. And although a wholesome diet may not cure every ailment, few diseases can be alleviated without it. Such a diet enables you to tap into the unlimited source of healing that permeates your body. It will help you enjoy greater energy, endurance, and strength, along with better skin quality and brighter eyes. When adopted with other lifestyle changes, it may allow you to effortlessly achieve a healthy weight. Your digestive system will be happy and function well. You will sleep soundly and wake up rested. As you begin to consume high-quality foods, you will also notice changes in your mental state, such as a greater ability to focus and be in the moment and a more creative and open mind. Emotionally, you may begin to prioritize honesty with yourself and others, and you may become more acutely aware that your feelings are a doorway to intuition. Your emotions are likely to flow more easily, and you'll have more direct access to an underlying level of peace. All of these physical, mental, and emotional changes will help you begin to connect more deeply with who you really are. Your true nature can shine freely through a clear body and mind.

Most of our food choices are emotionally driven, and making peace with food hinges on finding peace within ourselves. This is a lifelong journey, and as far as I can tell there are no shortcuts. Through my experience in the health field, I've come to understand that lasting change must come from a very deep level. It's not enough to change habits. We need to develop a deeper understanding and experience of how our food choices influence our physical, mental, emotional, and spiritual health. And then we need to expand our perspective to see that what we put on our plates directly affects not only ourselves but also the web of people, plants, creatures, and other elements of nature that come together to provide it for us.

When we eat "fake," or unnatural, foods, we become less authentic. When our foods are processed and fractionated, we become less centered. When we eat chemical residues that are designed to kill other life-forms, we die a little. When we eat food grown or raised with an element of human or animal suffering, we become hardened to our natural compassion for all life. When we choose foods solely for speed and convenience, we perpetuate the madness that rules our days.

Ultimately, eating is how we take in and transform the energies of the universe—energies that have been absorbed and stored by each vegetable, leaf, root, seed, nut, and fruit and released to us as a gift from nature. Once we experience the intimate relationship between our food choices, our bodies, our environment, and inner peace, making health-supporting choices becomes more effortless, joyful, and satisfying. When we begin to make food choices that affirm health, we say yes to all that is good. This is a path that can not only reduce illness but also foster more harmony within us, our families, and society.

The effects of food on our physical and psychospiritual health are immense, and I believe that many of these effects are as yet undiscovered by science. There are very few healing modalities that can affect us so significantly and consistently.

My Path to Health and Healing

The births of my children helped me see how deeply the ability to change is embedded in all of us. Through a natural opening of my heart to them, I received the gift of my own heart's unfolding, which continues to this day. This has served as a teacher for me, because I now see the potential for growth in everyone and have faith in the power of the soul to dislodge unconscious behavior. I'm not unique; I believe we all have the ability to transform and awaken from the metaphorical sleep of our former selves.

As I was nursing my son Jérémie, I began to plan for the day when I would eventually feed him solid foods. Like all parents, I wanted to offer my child the very best foundation for health. I also had an intuitive sense of the profound power of food. I took advantage of my time at home with Jérémie to read all I could about various nutritional approaches. One book that affected me profoundly was *Diet for a New America*, by John Robbins, heir to the Baskin-Robbins ice cream empire, who at age twenty-one decided to turn his back on the family business and seek out his own path. As I read his brilliant and courageous book on vegetarianism as an avenue to a more compassionate, healthful, and environmentally conscious way of life—for individuals and for society—I was devastated, inspired, educated, reborn, and, ultimately, transformed.

There was no turning back. In less than two weeks, my household was essentially vegan. Although I was excited about our new direction, it was challenging to make the transition from the traditional meat- and dairy-based diet I'd been raised on. Not only was there a new repertoire of foods to prepare, there were family members and friends to announce our decision to and concerns about our children's health to address. It was daunting.

Because we made such an extensive change so fast, every meal was an adventure—and some were certainly a challenge. I would look in the fridge and wonder what in the world I was going to make with "those vegetables." Eventually, thanks to the support of my former husband, to the information in magazines such as *Vegetarian Times*, and to some good cookbooks and helpful friends, I began to get the hang of the vegetarian lifestyle.

Better yet, with few exceptions the variety of new foods and flavors that we were exploring delighted us. I continued to read and educate myself, and food and nutrition became a new passion, eventually leading to a career as a holistic nutritionist and a position teaching for the Canadian School of Natural Nutrition. I soon learned that my early concerns about whether a vegetarian diet could be healthful were unfounded, coming from an ingrained but false belief that eating animal products was necessary for health. In the past twenty years, none of the members of my household have needed to take antibiotics or drugs of any kind, and we all enjoy excellent health. Moreover, both of my children are elite athletes.

Those dietary changes initiated shifts in virtually every area of my life. My interest in promoting health through lifestyle continued, and I was also drawn to holistic movement forms like yoga and therapeutic dance. The mental and emotional pieces of the health puzzle have become clearer over the years as my view of health broadened to include my whole being. This led to energy work, psychospiritual therapy, Buddhist-based mindfulness training, and an ever-deepening exploration of my true nature through meditation practice. I have rediscovered the freedom and joy of dancing, singing, playing the guitar, making pottery, drumming, gardening, spending time in nature, living sustainably, and growing some of our food. I am becoming more comfortable living in the magic of the unknown and look forward to a life of awakenings, synchronicities, laughter, service, and love. As you explore the information and recipes on these pages, may you recognize what you already deeply sense, thoroughly delight in your new food adventures, and continue to discover a life where joy flows and love abounds.

CHAPTER 1

Universal Dietary Principles

T he field of nutrition has become very complex, seemingly with as many approaches as there are experts, not to mention the unrelenting promotion of various supplements touted to be indispensable for health. Happily, I've found that sound nutritional principles are actually quite basic and easy to understand. If I had to condense all these principles into one unifying concept, I'd say that, to a large extent, everything we need for good health can be found in simple whole foods. That said, I do, of course, want to offer more specific guidance, and that is the topic of this chapter.

Making the Best Food Choices

As with everything in life, making the best choices leads to the best results. Based on personal experience, discussions with scores of students and clients, and the work of other holistic practitioners, I have found that certain dietary principles regarding daily food choices create clear health advantages for the majority of people, and that most of these principles also have enormous benefits beyond the health of the individual. I'll discuss each principle in detail, but for quick reference, here's a list:

- Eat whole foods that are as close to their natural state as possible.
- Eat a plant-based diet.
- Eat organic and biodynamic foods whenever possible.
- Focus on fresh foods.
- Try to eat local foods.
- Eat foods that are in season.
- Eat more raw foods.
- Eat a variety of foods, with different colors, flavors, textures, and shapes.
- Eat an alkalizing diet.
- Understand and respect your food sensitivities.
- Satisfy the subtle energetic needs of your body.
- Above all, eat consciously.

Eat Whole Foods

Healthy cells create healthy organs, healthy physiological systems, and a healthy body. In order for the trillions of cells in each human body to function optimally, we need the vitamins, minerals, proteins, fats, carbohydrates, water, fiber, and other nutrients that whole foods provide. Whenever foods are processed, many of their nutrients are lost or destroyed. For example, 80 percent of the minerals in rice are lost when the bran is removed during polishing to create white rice. Canned vegetables lose many of their heat-sensitive vitamins during processing. In addition, processed foods often contain chemical additives designed to "improve" flavor, texture, appearance, and shelf life—chemicals that are toxic to the body and may make you feel tired and sluggish.

In essence, whole foods are those that are closest to how they grow in nature. The less they have been tampered with between the field and your dinner table, the better. A food product sold in a box or package labeled with a long list of unpronounceable ingredients obviously isn't a whole food. But sometimes the distinction isn't as apparent. Fresh fruit has far more health benefits than fruit juice that has been pasteurized and canned or bottled. The process of juicing typically removes most or all of the fruit's fiber, and most of the vitamins are destroyed by heat and oxidation when the juice is packaged. Or consider wheat: Wheat berries, or whole kernels of wheat, are more wholesome than wheat bran or wheat germ on their own. The nutrients in whole wheat are packaged by nature and complement each other in perfect balance. Furthermore, when we consume refined foods, a "nutrient debt" is created in the body. For example, to make white sugar, sugar cane juice is boiled and crystallized, separating the nutrient-rich molasses from the nutrient-void sucrose (commonly know as white sugar). A nutrient debt is created as a result so that when we consume white sugar, the body draws from its own mineral stores in order to process the empty calories. Over time, this creates mineral deficiencies, which contribute to a host of health problems, including anemia, dental cavities, diabetes, hypoglycemia, obesity, and osteoporosis.

To receive the full benefit of the unsurpassed synergy of nutrients in whole foods, eat them as close as possible to how nature packaged them. Simply stated, center your diet primarily or solely on nutrient-dense fresh vegetables, fruits, grains, legumes, nuts, and seeds.

Eat a Plant-Based Diet

As I was growing up, I received endless social and cultural messages that the consumption of animal products is essential to health and well-being—as most everyone in Western society does. Standard approaches to eating, such as the four food groups and various versions of the food pyramid, which have been taught in schools and promoted by medical professionals, have long perpetuated the myth that a vegetarian or vegan diet is inadequate.

However, in reality the societies that enjoy the greatest health tend to eat diets that are predominantly plant-based, consisting of vegetables, fruits, grains, legumes, nuts, and seeds. The more animal products a culture consumes, the more degenerative diseases its population suffers. Four of the cultures with the greatest longevity are the Hunzas of Pakistan, the Abkhazians of Russia, the Vilcabambans of Ecuador, and the Okinawans of Japan. According to John Robbins in his book *Healthy at 100*, most of the people in these societies eat a diet that's 95 to 99 percent plant based. Rigorous studies support the link between a predominantly plant-based diet and superior health. For example, a long-term study by biochemist T. Colin Campbell, PhD, and colleagues (documented in his book *The China Study*) conclusively showed that as amounts of animal products in the diet increase, so does the incidence of a wide array of common degenerative diseases.

Every species is designed to eat certain foods. When given the choice, those species that aren't afflicted with advertising will eat basically the same diet day after day for a lifetime. What is the ideal diet for humans? Charles Darwin believed that humans are frugivores: animals that primarily eat fruit. Our DNA is 98 percent identical to that of the higher apes, who eat mostly fruit and tender greens. Furthermore, human anatomy and physiology are those of a natural vegetarian: nimble fingers for gathering; flat teeth and a jaw structured for grinding fruit and vegetables; a long, convoluted digestive system; digestive enzymes designed to break down complex carbohydrates; and a liver that can only process and excrete limited amounts of cholesterol, causing the remainder to be deposited in our tissues. So although we are capable of eating a wide variety of foods, not all of those foods are good for us.

Numerous studies have shown that people consuming the low-fat, high-fiber, plant-based diet that is natural for us live longer and have lower cholesterol levels, fewer heart attacks, and less risk of many forms of cancer than people who eat high quantities of meat, eggs, and dairy products. Those who eat a plant-based diet also are less prone to arthritis, constipation, diabetes, diverticulosis, gallstones, high blood pressure, kidney disease, kidney stones, multiple sclerosis, obesity, osteoporosis, and ulcers. Yet these diseases are on the rise in Western society. Astoundingly, a great deal of money and energy are devoted to researching procedures and medicines for fighting diet-associated diseases when a far simpler solution lies in prevention through a healthful lifestyle. Thankfully, increasing numbers of people are discovering the benefits of a wholesome plant-based diet and using this approach to reverse the course of lifestyle-related diseases.

A plant-based diet is also more compassionate. In order to supply meat and animal products at the rate that North Americans are consuming them, most food animals are raised on factory farms to maximize efficiency and profits. Little to no attention is paid to the fact that animals are sensitive creatures and capable of suffering. They are raised in cramped and unsuitable conditions, fed as cheaply as possible, and routinely given antibiotics and hormones. They are taken from their mothers at birth, and many never see the light of day. They routinely experience horrific procedures, such as debeaking and tail docking. They live surrounded by the stench of their own waste products and may live in cages stacked one on top of another. They are transported by truck and train in scorching heat and freezing cold and eventually lined up for slaughter, no doubt feeling immense terror as they smell and sense their impending death. My heart broke when I first read about this terrible mistreatment, and I wanted to make sure I didn't contribute to the ongoing suffering.

That said, in my experience as a nutritionist who often counsels people interested in a vegan diet, I've found that a gradual transition away from animal products works best for many people. One major reason for this is that adopting a plant-based diet often results in both a physical and an emotional detoxification (discussed in chapter 2). When people are making the transition, I encourage them to purchase animal products either at farmers' markets or at small family farms, seeking out farmers who raise their animals compassionately.

Reducing environmental impacts is also a compelling reason to eat a plant-based diet. When I first began researching vegetarianism, I was amazed to discover how environmentally destructive the typical North American meat-based diet is. A meat-centered diet can use up to forty times more fossil fuels—obviously making a significant contribution to global climate change. In fact, the United Nations Food and Agriculture Organization considers animal agriculture to be a larger contributor to global warming than the transportation sector.

The list of environmental insults is long, so I'll provide just a few more examples. Animal agriculture is responsible for 85 percent of topsoil loss. It is the main cause of destruction of tropical rain forests, which are decimated to provide land for grazing cattle for export to North America. Animal agriculture accounts for half of the fresh water used in North America and produces an obscene amount of manure, which is the top source of organic water pollution in North America. It is an inefficient use of land, requiring fifteen acres annually to raise food for a person eating a meat-centered diet, but only one acre annually to grow food for someone on a plant-based diet. When you put all of this together, it's obvious that shifting people's orientation to a plant-based diet would have enormous environmental benefits. Among other things, it would free up land to plant trees that could absorb carbon dioxide, provide us with oxygen, stabilize the topsoil, and offer valuable wildlife habitat.

Eat Organic and Biodynamic Foods

Organic farmers use no synthetic pesticides, herbicides, fungicides, or fertilizers. Therefore, these chemicals are not present in organic produce, easing the work of the liver, which tends to be overburdened by the many toxins we're exposed to in this modern world. It doesn't require deep reflection to see that we cannot continue to expose our food to chemicals that are designed to kill life and expect our bodies to remain unaffected. These chemicals are accumulating in our rivers, lakes, oceans, soil, and land, and also in plants and animals (including us humans), slowly poisoning the planet we rely on to sustain us.

Organic farming practices also help maintain and even improve the quality of the topsoil, which is a complex living ecosystem made up of insects, microorganisms, fungi, humus, and more. Globally, over one-third of croplands are losing topsoil more quickly than it is naturally generated. Organic farmers reverse this dynamic by replenishing the soil with manure, compost, and rock dust.

This ongoing commitment to give back to the earth has measurable positive effects. Research has shown that crops grown by organic farmers tend to have a higher mineral content. (Interestingly, minerals are the only nutrient other than water that plants draw from the earth.) Minerals are essential to the structure of the human body and virtually every bodily function, including the assimilation of other nutrients.

It follows that foods grown in healthy soil will be more robust and flavorful. Many top chefs know this and insist on organic (and locally grown) ingredients.

So when you buy organic produce, you're supporting farmers who are committed to maintaining the quality of the soil our food is grown in and minimizing their negative impacts on the natural world. They also tend to grow more varieties of crops, many of them not favored in conventional agriculture. Some of these varieties of plants have been used as food crops since ancient times, and many of them yield produce that has greater nutritional value than modern, hybridized versions. In addition, these plants are often naturally hardy and don't require synthetic chemicals to fight off insects and weeds.

Another benefit of purchasing organic produce is that it's currently the best way to be sure you aren't getting genetically modified foods. In the United States and Canada, genetically modified foods and products that contain them cannot be labeled "organic." Genetically modified organisms (GMOs) have had their DNA artificially manipulated by a variety of techniques. Production of GMO foods has become quite common since the mid-1990s, including some important food crops, such as soybeans and corn. Studies of laboratory animals have indicated that consuming genetically modified foods may cause adverse health effects.

Another concern is that GMO crops can cross-pollinate with non-GMO plants and spread the engineered genes. It is believed that GMOs have a negative effect on other forms of life, including insects (particularly bees), as well as soil organisms. Finally, GMO seed is patented by the large agrochemical companies that produce it, making it illegal for farmers to save seeds to grow another crop (something farmers have traditionally done for centuries). This forces farmers to purchase their seed from these companies, creating an ongoing dependency that leaves the farmers around the world (notably in India, as well as in other countries) financially bereft, while benefiting corporate agriculture. For these and many other reasons, several countries have banned GMO crops or seeds or are proposing to do so.

Focus on Fresh Foods

The closer produce is to being freshly harvested, the better. Nutrients and life force begin to decrease from the moment fruits and vegetables are picked. For this reason, many people are drawn to growing some of their own food or purchasing it from local farmers or farmers' markets.

After harvest, some foods lose their nutrients more quickly than others. For example, the vitamins in leafy greens deteriorate quite rapidly, whereas the vitamins in root vegetables hold up for a longer period of time. In practical terms, this means you should eat greens soon after purchase, whereas you can make dishes with root vegetables a few days later.

Ideally, fruit should be picked when it's ripe, as this is when its nutrient levels and digestibility are the highest. However, ripe fruit is less able to withstand the rigors of transportation or the lag time between harvest and purchase. Therefore, fruit picked at the peak of ripeness is rarely found in supermarkets. Choose ripe, local fruit when possible, and when that isn't possible, allow fruit to ripen at room temperature before eating it.

When it's necessary to preserve food, the best choices are cold-cellar storage, dehydrating, or fermenting. These all have a minimum negative effect on nutrient levels. In fact, fermenting actually increases the amounts of some nutrients, including B vitamins.

Try to Eat Local Foods

I love shopping at my local farmers' market and try to get there early in the morning so I have access to the best selection. The freshness and flavor of the food is unsurpassed, and the sense of community and connection with farmers and vendors is an added pleasure. I enjoy the details that local farmers include on their signs alongside the prices, such as "Celery seedlings started on my kitchen counter in March," "Beans picked last night in the rain," or "Baby bok choy grown by my neighbor in a greenhouse warmed by a woodstove" (the latter in February). These tidbits enhance the process of shopping for produce and preparing it in my kitchen later on.

Purchasing locally grown food has many benefits. It supports the local economy and small family farms, which protects fertile land from being developed. It also allows people who have farming in their blood to do what they love and make a living at it. It's a mutually supportive endeavor that nurtures a sense of human connection that is essential to emotional health.

Choosing local produce also encourages the cultivation of plant varieties that are high in nutrition and flavor but don't necessarily travel well. Because of the decreased transportation distance, local food tends to be fresher when it gets to the market. Of course, a huge downside to transporting food long distances by truck, train, or plane is the enormous carbon footprint. In addition, it's extremely unlikely that locally grown food is irradiated—a common practice at international borders when foods are imported.

There are many ways to support local foods. You can grow some of your own produce or join a community garden if you don't have a yard or area suitable for gardening. You can shop at your local farmers' market or buy into a local farm's harvest by participating in community supported agriculture. At the minimum, read the signs and stickers on the produce at your grocery store and make your choices accordingly.

Eat Foods That Are in Season

As mentioned earlier, freshly harvested ripe foods are at their peak nutritionally. In addition, dietary needs vary according to the seasons. If you pay attention to your body's signals, you'll find that the types of food that bring you satisfaction are different in the spring, summer, fall, and winter. Seasonal eating is easy and intuitive when you buy locally grown produce.

As a bonus, eating with the seasons is likely to bring variety and adventure to your diet. Committing to seasonal foods will inspire you to expand your gastronomical horizons as you experiment with the current bounty. You're likely to get acquainted with some unfamiliar root vegetables that your great-grandparents probably knew well. You'll also learn about nutritious greens of every sort and start to experiment with foods you may never have known about or considered consuming before. Another upside to eating produce that's in season is that it tends to be more reasonably priced.

Eat More Raw Foods

A nutritional approach that can help foster both health and peace is eating more raw and living foods. When you think about it, all creatures consume their foods in a raw state except for humans and their companion animals, both of which are vastly more plagued by degenerative diseases than any other creatures on the planet. Clearly there's a connection.

Raw foods typically have the highest levels of nutrients. While cooking wisely with heat (steaming for a few minutes, for instance) can make some foods more digestible and some nutrients more available, high-heat cooking methods such as frying and broiling destroy many nutrients. Proteins, carbohydrates, and fatty acids are all damaged, sometimes producing carcinogenic compounds in the process. Vitamins are often destroyed, minerals can be lost in cooking liquids, and fiber becomes softer and a less effective intestinal cleanser.

Incorporate more raw foods into your diet by eating more fresh fruits and vegetables. For example, you might start your day with a fresh fruit salad followed by a large green smoothie, or you could center at least one meal a day around a big salad full of fresh, raw ingredients. Try to include at least one raw food with every meal, and consider juicing fruits and vegetables at home so you can enjoy the benefits of truly fresh juice.

Eat a Wide Variety of Foods

Besides adding interest to your daily meals, eating a wide variety of foods provides a broad range of nutrients and helps prevent the development of food sensitivities. Experiment and expand the types of greens, vegetables, fruits, grains, legumes, nuts, and seeds that you consume. When looking to diversify your diet, consider colors, flavors, textures, and even shapes.

When you eat foods from the entire color spectrum over the course of the day, you're adding more to your diet than just visual appeal. You're ensuring that you naturally obtain a wider range of nutrients, along with a wider range of the subtle energetic qualities foods contain. Eat red apples, beets, bell peppers, and tomatoes; orange apricots, carrots, peaches, winter squash, and yams; yellow bell peppers, corn, lemons, and summer squash; green broccoli, honeydew melons, kale, lettuce, parsley, spinach, and leafy greens in general; and blue and purple berries, cabbage, eggplant, grapes, and plums. Don't overlook white and beige—colors that take in not just cauliflower, onions, and potatoes but also many beans, grains, nuts, and seeds.

Also aim for a diversity of flavors. The human palate is able to detect six distinct tastes: sweet, sour, salty, bitter, astringent, and pungent. Many ancient healing modalities maintain that these flavors have psychospiritual qualities. To be balanced physically and spiritually, it's a good idea to include all of them in your diet on a daily basis, preferably at each meal. Although most whole foods have a blend of these flavors, one is usually predominant:

- Sweet foods include sweet fruits, such as bananas, dates, figs, and melons; most grains, including rice and wheat; sweet vegetables, such as beets and carrots; many nuts; and, of course, maple syrup and sugarcane.
- Sour foods include grapes, lemons, plums, and other sour fruits, as well as tomatoes (actually another fruit), cultured vegetables, and vinegar.
- Salty foods include celery, some leafy greens, sea vegetables, and any food with added salt.
- Bitter foods include all green leafy vegetables, such as chicory, collard greens, endive, kale, lettuce, mustard greens, and Swiss chard, and also cilantro and parsley.
- Astringency is not so much a flavor as a sensation of dryness in the mouth. It occurs when you consume apples, beans, broccoli, cabbage, cauliflower, lentils, pears, potatoes, sprouts, and some nuts.
- Pungent foods include cayenne, chilies, garlic, ginger, leeks, onions, radishes, and spicy foods in general.

Here are some examples of how you can balance all six of these tastes in a single dish: In a pasta dish, the pasta has an inherent sweetness that's well complemented by astringent Roman beans, bitter rapini, pungent garlic, salt, and sour tomatoes. In an Asian meal, complement sweet rice with astringent broccoli, bitter bok choy, pungent ginger, salty tamari, and sour rice vinegar. In a salad, build on a base of bitter lettuce, adding astringent sunflower sprouts, pungent red onions, salt, sour cider vinegar, and a little sweet maple syrup. Many of the recipes in this book feature these sorts of combinations, containing contain all six flavors within a single dish. You'll notice that these sorts of dishes tend to be more satisfying, and with time, you'll probably begin to intuitively and naturally add all six tastes when cooking (if you don't already).

Another way of adding variety to your diet and making food more satisfying is to include a range of textures: for example, soft, ripe bananas and peaches; crunchy apples, nuts, and raw vegetables; chewy grains, such as short-grain brown rice; juicy melons and tomatoes; smooth blended smoothies and soups; granular flaxseeds, hempseeds, and sesame seeds; and rich, creamy nut milks. Lastly, don't overlook shape as a way to diversify your diet. Foods can be eaten whole, diced, sliced, cut into matchsticks, grated, blended, or puréed. Improving your knife skills (and having the right equipment, as discussed on pages 187 to 188) will go a long way toward adding creativity and interest to your meals. Also enjoy the visual feast of the different shapes whole foods naturally have, from slender grains of wild rice to small, spherical chickpeas, and from asparagus spears to ever-appealing broccoli trees.

Eat an Alkaline Diet

To maintain a healthy balance, the human body should be in a slightly alkaline state. Disease tends to develop in an acid environment, and most conditions heal in an alkaline environment. In order to keep the body's pH at an optimum level (blood pH levels of 7.3 to 7.4), we need to consume about 75 percent vegetables, fruits, and sprouts, which are the alkalizing food groups. The other 25 percent of the diet can consist of a variety of high-quality whole foods from categories such as beans, grains, and nuts. Put simply, about three-quarters of your plate should be vegetables and fruits in order to maintain a health-sustaining alkaline state. The recipes and suggestions in this book reflect this recommendation and will give you plenty of ideas for incorporating more vegetables and fruit into your diet.

Interestingly, while nuts, seeds, grains, and legumes are somewhat acid-forming, they are less so when grown organically, as this gives them a higher mineral content. (Minerals tend to be alkalizing.) Soaking and especially sprouting will also make them less acid forming.

Understand and Respect Your Food Sensitivities

On a daily basis, many of us eat foods that our bodies are sensitive to or allergic to. Many people are unaware that consuming these foods can contribute to physical discomforts such as bloating, fatigue, frequent illness, inflammation, skin issues, sleep disturbances, and weight gain. The most common food sensitivities are to caffeine, citrus, corn, dairy, eggs, gluten, some nuts, peanuts, red meat, soy, and wheat. If you have food sensitivities, these symptoms won't be alleviated until you stop eating the problematic foods. Once your body has healed, you may be able to add limited amounts of those foods back into your diet, providing that you choose high-quality versions of them, such as ripe organic citrus fruits, organic corn, soaked raw nuts, or soaked or sprouted grains.

Gluten, which is a common cause of food sensitivities and allergies, is a protein contained in many grains. It's particularly prevalent in wheat but is also present in barley, Kamut, rye, spelt, and triticale. It may also be found in oats, but this is due to cross-contamination at the processing plant from wheat and other grains that contain gluten. Gluten can be very difficult for some people to digest and can lead to or exacerbate digestive disturbances, promote inflammation, and actually damage the intestinal wall. It can also cause behavioral issues in children and emotional imbalances in adults.

I recommend that everyone eat a wide variety of gluten-free grains, such as brown rice, quinoa, millet, wild rice, buckwheat, teff, and amaranth. Gluten-free grains provide a wonderful base for stir-fries, stews, and curries. You can also substitute gluten-free flours for some or all of the wheat flour in recipes for baked goods. However, this can affect flavor, texture, and other qualities, so you might want to follow some gluten-free recipes or read up on the topic before experimenting extensively.

It's also helpful to soak or sprout grains before consuming them, particularly those that contain gluten, as gluten is partially broken down by these processes. Soaking and sprouting also substantially increase the availability of nutrients in grains. When shopping for bread, tortillas, and other such products, be on the lookout for varieties made from sprouted grains, as these are increasingly available.

Satisfy the Subtle Energetic Needs of Your Body

Beyond giving us nutrients, foods offer subtle energetic qualities. Think of foods as having personalities. When you eat them, you absorb some of their personality into your system.

Greens, such as collard greens, kale, lettuce, mustard greens, spinach, and Swiss chard, tend to be expansive and add lightness, vitality, renewal, and clarity to the body. They also provide impressive quantities of vitamins and minerals.

Root vegetables, such as beets, carrots, celery root, ginger, Jerusalem artichokes, parsnips, radishes, rutabagas, and turnips, are a crucial but often overlooked component of a nutritious, balanced diet. Whereas most other vegetables are expansive and can leave you feeling a little spacey, root vegetables provide much-needed grounding, helping you feel settled, centered, and focused. They are also warming. Isn't it perfect that they're most readily available in the fall, just as the weather starts to turn colder? And because they keep well for months, you can add them to salads, soups, and stews throughout the winter.

Fruits have a high water content, are easy to digest, and have the most pleasing flavors of all foods. They bring sweetness, delight, and a sense of freedom, and support spiritual and artistic endeavors.

Legumes and grains are dense, hearty, warming foods. They can help you feel nourished, confident, cared for, and purposeful. If you're transitioning to a plant-based diet, they can also replace the subtle energies that you're accustomed to obtaining from animal foods.

Nuts and seeds are rich sources of fats and protein and can promote strength and add weight. When eaten in moderation, they are physically and emotionally satisfying, and create warmth and lubrication. In excess they tend to overwork the liver and digestive system in general. Specific recommendations are discussed on page 17.

Eat Consciously

The ideal way to create a diet that will give you optimum health, vitality, and longevity is to become more conscious of how your food choices affect all aspects of your life. Your body will help you individualize your approach to eating by giving you a wide variety of signals about the best nutritional choices for you personally. You are the best expert about yourself. All you have to do is listen as attentively as possible.

True listening means being open, receptive, and curious. It helps greatly to be present in your body as you eat, which means eating without distractions. That way your body can communicate with you through sensation. The more you pay attention and practice awareness, the more attuned you'll be to the effects of foods on your being, including the subtle energetic effects discussed above. In addition, and although you may find this surprising, sometimes it's helpful to drop all the rules you've accumulated about a "proper" diet and to simply eat whatever your body is asking for—with awareness.

I suggest keeping a food log for a while. Begin to notice and write down how your daily food choices affect you. For example, are there correlations between what you eat and how easy it is to fall asleep at night and stay asleep, and how rested you feel the next morning? Examine how your face looks in the morning. Processed foods and even whole foods that you're sensitive to will tend to make your eyes dull and your skin pasty and may cause your tongue to be coated with a heavy white film. You might also notice that certain foods make your joints feel stiff or lead to a stuffy or runny nose. Also note how food you ate the previous day affects your emotions the next morning, including your enthusiasm for the day ahead of you.

Over the course of the day, you might feel differences in your energy levels before and after eating. Also notice whether certain foods cause allergic reactions, bloating, indigestion, sleepiness, a reduced ability to make sound decisions, or a lack of focus and centeredness. Be sure to attend to how hungry you feel prior to eating and whether you were distracted while eating. Did you enjoy your meal? Did it leave you feeling satisfied? Do you feel any guilt, unhappiness, boredom, or confusion?

One of the best indicators of how well your diet is suited to your body is how well your food is digested. The number and quality of bowel movements you have over the course of a day is a good indicator here. On a healthful plant-based diet, you will generally have a bowel movement first thing in the morning after a glass or two of water or after breakfast. If you eat a satisfying lunch and dinner composed of whole foods, you'll probably have a bowel movement within half an hour after each meal. These bowel movements will be large and easy to eliminate. They will be medium to dark brown in color and solid but fluffy, not hard. They will tend to float and will often begin to fall apart as you flush the toilet.

You are the only inhabitant of your body, and therefore (potentially) its best observer. It's important that you trust what your body is telling you about how it wants to be cared for. Filter any advice or external information about diet through your wisdom, your heart, and your intuition. Apply what feels right for you now, and let the rest fall into place as it will. The pursuit of health and a healthful lifestyle is a fascinating and never-ending journey that will bring you rewards beyond measure.

Supplementing a Whole-Foods Diet

Many people wonder whether they'll need to take supplements to ensure adequate nutrition when eating a plant-based diet. Eating a wide variety of high-quality whole foods should more than suffice. This is truly the best route to radiant health. The nutrients found within whole foods work synergistically and often occur in balanced amounts and highly absorbable forms and therefore provide optimum nutrition.

Still, you might be inclined to take supplements of isolated nutrients, such as vitamins and minerals. I recommend against it for the following reasons:

- Taking supplements consisting of isolated nutrients often causes imbalances of other nutrients within the body. For example, excess iron can block zinc absorption, and too much calcium can create an imbalance with manganese and magnesium levels.

- Getting more of any given nutrient isn't necessarily better. The body needs only what it can effectively absorb. The excessive amounts of vitamins and minerals found in many supplements must be excreted by the body, potentially overloading the organs of elimination with an avoidable task.

- Some lower-quality brands of supplements contain nutrients in forms that are inexpensive but not easily absorbed by the human body.

- All physiological functions of the human body require dozens if not hundreds of nutrients, not just those currently understood and designated as "essential." For example, taking iron for anemia is only one very small piece of the puzzle. Other nutrients are involved, such as those that play a role in red blood cell formation (essential fatty acids, molybdenum, vitamin B_{12}, and others), and the body's ability to absorb these nutrients through the digestive tract is also an issue. Whole foods have a variety of nutrients in an inherent balance and are therefore more able to compensate for deficiencies.

- Supplements can be very expensive. Money is better spent on high-quality whole foods.

All of that said, there are a few reasons why you might want to take supplements:

- You're changing your diet and just starting to learn about whole foods and therefore feel that supplements will make up for any gaps during the transition.

- You eat out at restaurants fairly often and are uncertain about the nutritional value in the foods you're choosing.

- You're concerned about getting enough vitamin B_{12}, which is often deficient in plant-based diets. Most experts recommend a vitamin B_{12} supplement for vegans.

- You don't get outside in the sun very often and are concerned about your vitamin D status.

Should you choose to take supplements, ask a trusted holistic nutritionist for advice on the best brands and make sure the nutrients they contain come from natural sources. Also pay attention to how you feel when taking supplements. When you no longer need a particular supplement, you may feel unwell after taking it, begin to feel averse to taking it, or consistently forget to take it. These can be subconscious signals from your body.

Fresh Juices

Freshly pressed juices are, in my opinion, the ultimate supplement to any diet. Most of us are deficient in minerals because agricultural soils have become depleted of these nutrients and because the stress of modern life takes a toll on our bodies. Fresh juices, which provide abundant minerals, can be part of the solution. Because they are made from whole foods, they have an ideal balance of nutrients, and those nutrients will be absorbed from the stomach and small intestine minutes after ingestion. This is important, as many people's digestive systems are overworked and fatigued due to years of poor eating and unmanaged stress. Saturating your cells with a rich supply of nutrients without taxing your digestive system is rejuvenating for your whole body. Most people will feel the energizing effects of juice soon after drinking it and, within a week of drinking fresh juices, will notice an increase in energy levels in general.

People often ask what kind of juicer is best. Cost can be a factor if you're on a budget. Many are priced as low as $100. The upside of these juicers is that they are less expensive. The downside is that they may use friction to produce the juice, which heats the produce and destroys nutrients. Of course, you'll want to extract as much juice as possible from the ingredients you use; however, many of the less-expensive juicers leave the pulp quite moist. If you find this to be the case, try feeding the pulp back through the juicer. For further recommendations for juicers, see page 188.

Probiotics

Another helpful type of supplement is health-promoting friendly bacteria, or probiotics. The human gut, in particular the colon, houses many strains of bacteria, called intestinal flora, and a number of these are absolutely essential for our health.

Intestinal bacteria play many important roles, including helping to break down undigested food particles and neutralizing toxins. They prevent the overgrowth of disease-causing microbes, including fungi and yeasts, in part by acidifying the bowel environment. All of these functions help maintain the integrity of the intestinal tract, which is extremely important for maintaining the strength of the immune system. In addition, health-promoting intestinal flora produce B vitamins, vitamin K, and substances that fight unfriendly bacteria. They also make up half of the dry mass of feces, thereby helping with elimination and detoxification (the process of neutralizing or transforming toxic substances or removing them from the body).

Most people have greatly reduced gut flora due to taking antibiotics and other drugs, drinking chlorinated water, and eating processed foods. It's important to replenish intestinal flora by taking probiotic supplements or, even better, consuming fermented or cultured foods such as kefir, yogurt, and unpasteurized sauerkraut and miso.

Superfood Powders

Superfood powders, commonly added to green smoothies, are a popular way to supplement a whole-foods diet. If you aren't drinking fresh juices regularly and aren't consistently using organic produce, supplementing with superfood powders is probably a good idea.

Superfood powders are primarily made from dried foods that are known to contain high concentrations of a wide variety of nutrients, particularly vitamins, minerals, proteins, and essential fatty acids. Examples include the juice of grasses such as alfalfa, barley, and wheat; algae such as blue-green algae, chlorella, and spirulina; and finely ground seeds such as chia, flax, and hemp. Many manufacturers offer formulas that contain a variety of ingredients, including grass powders, algae, fruit and vegetable powders, herbs, medicinal mushrooms, and probiotics.

If you choose to supplement with a superfood powder, I recommend that you seek the advice of a nutritionist to help guide your choice of products. However, I will share a few pointers. When purchasing superfood powders, single-ingredient powders (including those in tablet and capsule form) are often the best way to ensure high concentrations of a particular food and its nutrients. They are also usually more cost-effective. Plus, powders with multiple ingredients are often proprietary formulas, and if you react to one of these products, it can be difficult to determine the exact cause of the sensitivity. Beware of inexpensive fillers like lecithin, pectin, and rice bran, which are included in an attempt to fool you into thinking that you're getting more nutrients than you actually are. Also note that some powders include so-called natural flavorings. Many people quickly become tired of the taste of these.

I have some reservations about the addition of herbs to superfood powders. First, we don't all have the same needs; which herbs are appropriate depends on the individual's constitution and current state of health. Second, it's best to take most herbs only for a short time. The body develops a tolerance to the active substances in a given herb, and then it no longer has the same effect.

Antinutrients

Clearly, it's important to choose fresh, high-quality whole foods to ensure good digestion and to supplement with fresh juices, probiotics, and possibly superfood powders. It's also helpful to consider factors that destroy nutrients in the foods you eat and factors that either cause you to excrete excessive quantities of nutrients or prevent you from absorbing nutrients. Any influence that depletes your overall levels of nutrients can be considered an antinutrient.

Some common antinutrients are physical, mental, and emotional stress; lack of exercise or sleep; eating refined and processed foods, such as white sugar, white flour, soft drinks, and fried foods; smoking; consumption of caffeine, animal protein, or alcohol; many prescription drugs, especially antibiotics and birth control pills, and also recreational drugs and even some supplements; overeating; and exposure to chemicals from various sources. You would do well to avoid these as much as possible.

Reenvisioning the Food Groups for Optimum Health

The following guidelines for daily food choices are based on my personal experience, my work with students and clients, information from like-minded health experts, and personal research. They are, by necessity, general. Make adjustments as needed for your situation, including any dietary restrictions you may have because of illness or food sensitivities. However, for most people these guidelines can serve as an excellent foundation for a diet that will promote health and longevity.

The percentages for each food group refer to the approximate volume of food, as opposed to calories. I believe you don't need to be concerned about calories when consuming a whole-foods diet that encourages body-led food choices. I haven't included serving sizes in these recommendations (other than some suggestions for foods with a high fat content) because appropriate serving size varies from person to person depending on size, activity level, overall health, stage of life, and other factors. Try listening to your body to determine when you've eaten enough of a certain food. When you eat with awareness, any given food will be appealing and tasty as long as your body is receptive to it. Once you've eaten all of that food you need for the day, it will become less appealing.

VEGETABLES: 50 PERCENT OR MORE OF FOOD INTAKE

- Include at least two green vegetables (broccoli, kale, lettuce, spinach, Swiss chard, and so on) and one orange vegetable (carrots, winter squash, sweet potatoes, and so on) every day.
- Favor nonstarchy vegetables like leafy greens, broccoli, cauliflower, celery, and cucumber, and low-starch vegetables like beets, carrots, and winter squash, over higher starch vegetables like potatoes and sweet potatoes.
- Include a wide variety of vegetables, preferably organic.
- Generally choose fresh vegetables, rather than canned or frozen.
- Focus on vegetables that are in season.
- Include some raw vegetables every day, on their own, in smoothies, or in salads.
- Include sprouts and sea vegetables several times a week.

FRUIT: 10 TO 25 PERCENT OF FOOD INTAKE

- Include at least two different fruits every day.
- Include a variety of fruits, preferably organic.
- Generally choose fresh fruits, rather than canned or frozen.
- Focus on ripe fruits that are in season.

WHOLE GRAINS: 10 TO 25 PERCENT OF FOOD INTAKE

- Focus on intact whole grains, as opposed to flours and other processed grains.
- Eat a variety of gluten-free grains: brown rice, quinoa, millet, buckwheat, teff, and amaranth.
- Choose more alternatives to wheat. If gluten isn't an issue, this can include grains such as Kamut, rye, and spelt.
- Soak whole grains for four to eight hours prior to cooking.
- Choose sprouted-grain products.
- Choose gluten-free whole-grain pastas, made with brown rice or buckwheat, for example.
- Eat less grain if that improves your digestion and overall health. You can replace it with more fruit and starchy vegetables like winter squash and sweet potatoes.

CONCENTRATED PROTEINS: 10 TO 20 PERCENT OF FOOD INTAKE

- Eat legumes (chickpeas, kidney beans, lentils, split peas, and so on) at least once every day.
- Eat tofu and tempeh up to three times per week if you like, if soy isn't problematic for you. Choose organic varieties and opt for tofu made from sprouted soybeans when possible.

- Be aware that vegetables, especially green leafy vegetables, are a good source of protein if eaten in sufficient quantities.
- Add sprouts (alfalfa, broccoli, buckwheat, clover, lentil, mung bean, sunflower, and so on) to salads and other dishes.

FATS AND OILS: 5 PERCENT OF FOOD INTAKE

- Eat a maximum of ¼ cup to ½ cup of raw nuts and seeds (almonds, cashews, pecans, walnuts, and so on, and pumpkin, sesame, sunflower, and other seeds) daily. Purchase only whole nuts, as they tend to be fresher; chopping or grinding them increases their exposure to air, which speeds rancidity.
- Eat 1 to 3 tablespoons of chia seeds, flaxseeds, or hempseeds a few times per week, adding them to smoothies or sprinkling them on cooked grains, salads, and vegetable dishes. As with nuts, purchase only whole seeds.
- Optionally, eat a maximum of 1 tablespoon of raw nut or seed butter each day.
- Optionally, include a maximum of 1 to 2 tablespoons of cold-pressed oil (coconut, flax, hemp, olive, and sesame) every day. Use any of these in salad dressings or drizzled over cooked foods that won't be reheated. When cooking over heat, use only coconut, olive, or sesame oil.
- Optionally, eat fat-rich fruits (avocado and olives) once per day.

The Most Healthful Oils

Whenever using oil in food preparation, be sure to use cold-pressed or extra-virgin oil. This means the nut, seed, or olive is simply pressed to extract the oil with no added heat, chemicals, or other procedures. Flaxseed and hempseed oil can be found in the refrigerated section of natural food stores, and olive, sesame, and coconut oil will be on the shelves with the rest of the oils.

Water

- Drink about six to ten 8-ounce glasses of water a day.
- Realize that water needs vary depending on exercise levels and temperature, as well as dietary factors, such as the quantity of water-rich foods, salt, caffeinated beverages, and alcohol consumed.
- Drink filtered or purified water.
- Consider drinking remineralized and alkalized water, because they are most similar to spring water, nature's best water offering, and contribute to maintaining a health-promoting pH level in the body.

Harvest Fruit Salad, *page 42*

Veggie Pâté on yam slices, *page 76*

CHAPTER 2

Beyond Diet:
Digestion and Detoxification

T he term "diet" refers to what you put into your mouth, whereas "nutrition" is what actually gets into the trillions of cells in your body. Two main factors both enable and potentially limit the quantity of nutrients your diet provides: your ability to digest the food you eat and the toxic load your body must process.

Digestion: Transforming Diet into Nutrition

Most people actually digest very little of what they eat because their digestive systems have been compromised by years of eating poor-quality foods and living with high levels of unmanaged stress. Food that isn't digested properly ferments in the intestine, introduces toxins into the bloodstream, feeds fungi and parasites, and creates layers of buildup on the intestinal wall (called mucoid plaque), further decreasing absorption. As important as it is to purchase and prepare high-quality foods, it's equally important to ensure proper absorption of those foods. Here are some guidelines to help you build more "digestive fire" (that is, a strong, healthy metabolism) so that the food you consume is more thoroughly absorbed and used.

Keep Meals Simple and Be Careful of Certain Food Combinations

If you experience digestive discomfort or problems, you may be eating combinations of foods that don't work well for you. Sometimes mono meals (eating just one type of food at a meal) can be much easier to digest. For starters, try eating simpler meals and see for yourself how much better you feel. You don't have to get all of your required nutrients at one meal. You can satisfy your nutritional needs by eating a variety of high-quality foods over several days or the course of a week.

Many people find that eating fruit with denser foods can be problematic. Fruit is digested quickly, but this process will be held up if it's mixed with denser proteins, starches, and fats. Eating fruit after a big meal can be particularly troublesome. The fruit tends to ferment as it sits in the stomach waiting for the meal to pass through, causing bloating and gas.

As a rule, for smooth digestion it's best to eat fruit by itself or with vegetables that have a high water content, such as celery, cucumber, lettuce, and other greens. If you find that eating a snack of fruit causes your blood sugar to rise excessively, try eating it with water-rich vegetables. Mixing fruit with greens in a smoothie is a great way to get this combination. Personally, I find that small amounts of fruit in a vegetable salad pose no problems. Although the combination of fruit and fat can be problematic, it's often a question of quantities. Eating a small handful of almonds with an apple may be fine, whereas a larger quantity of almonds is a recipe for gas later on. As always, listen to your body and gain insight from experience.

The other main guideline for food combining is to avoid mixing concentrated proteins and starches at a meal. If you're transitioning to a plant-based diet or simply increasing the amount of legumes in your diet, start with small portions of legumes at first. Eating legumes primarily with vegetables, rather than grains, can also ease digestion. If you feel more satisfied when eating legumes with grains, include only one grain or carbohydrate in the meal; for example, eat beans with a little brown rice and a salad, but not with bread or winter squash as well. See pages 181 to 182 for more specific guidelines for cooking and increasing the digestibility of legumes.

Eat Only When Hungry

Eating when you aren't hungry is like throwing too much wood on a fire. It can smother the digestive fire and overwork the whole system. Rather than eating by the clock, take time to listen to your hunger signals. This may mean skipping a meal or eating less than usual sometimes. Here are some indicators you can use as clues: You'll know you're truly hungry if you salivate freely at the thought or sight of food. Another indicator is feeling the hunger signal, which is felt as an empty sensation at the back of the throat, not in the stomach. When your stomach feels relaxed and receptive, that's also an indicator of true hunger.

Eat in a Calm, Relaxed State

Eating when you feel calm and relaxed is one of the most effective things you can do to enhance digestion, yet simply wanting to relax doesn't always work. Most of us have patterns of stress built into our lives and ingrained habits of holding tension, so it takes steady practice and dedication to gradually unwind. Nonetheless, this is a worthwhile and profoundly beneficial undertaking for many reasons.

With respect to digestion, all of the functions of the digestive system—including the secretion of saliva and pancreatic juice, the absorption of nutrients through the intestinal wall, and the work of the liver and kidneys—are governed by the parasympathetic nervous system. This system regulates the internal organs and operates without any conscious effort on our part when we are in a relaxed state. The other branch of the autonomic nervous system, called the sympathetic nervous system, governs the stress response, also known as the fight, flight, or freeze response. When the sympathetic nervous system is on high alert, the functions governed by the parasympathetic system are suppressed. So when you're operating under stress, your digestion is compromised. If, like most people, you spend much time in some degree of stress, thereby leading to arousal of the sympathetic nervous system, you need to develop the ability to easily shift back into parasympathetic mode.

It takes time and practice to unwind back to this natural state. The most beneficial way to do so is to engage in daily practices that bring you to an ever-deepening state of relaxation, such as body-based meditation, yoga, conscious movement, and spending time in nature. In this way, the pathways that turn on the parasympathetic nervous system, and thereby enhance relaxation and digestion, will be more available when you sit down to eat your meals.

Eat Mindfully

Practice conscious eating, connecting to the food with all of your senses and a grateful attitude. This requires eating without the distractions of a phone, computer, television, reading material, or loud music. Sit down and slow down. Appreciate the appearance, aromas, flavors, colors, textures, and other aspects of the food you're eating. This makes eating a richer, more fulfilling experience that transcends simply filling your stomach.

Gratitude opens your heart and your entire being to receiving and creates an attitude where it is possible to consistently make health-supporting choices and feel satisfied with less. When you eat consciously and truly enjoy the experience, you'll find it easier to let go of any battles with food that you are struggling with.

If you're used to eating with distractions, eating mindfully will be a challenge at first. It's normal to find it difficult to slow down. However, as with any good relationship, having a healthy relationship with food requires honesty and attention. So allow yourself to be present with the discomfort of being undistracted as you eat. It will pass, as all things do, making room for the possibility of connection and deep satisfaction.

Chew Thoroughly

Chewing your food to a paste breaks it down into very small particles. Because these particles have a small volume, most of their nutrients are at or near the surface and therefore more accessible to digestive enzymes along the length of the digestive system. Digestive enzymes break these particles into even smaller components so they can be absorbed and utilized by the cells. Large chunks of unchewed food, on the other hand, often pass through the intestine with most of their volume untouched by digestive secretions. Therefore their nutrients are largely unabsorbed. Another benefit to chewing thoroughly is that this mixes the food with saliva, which lubricates its passage through the digestive system, and enzymes that begin to break down starches. It's also important to mix juices and smoothies with the saliva in your mouth, so drink them slowly and "chew" each mouthful.

Avoid Drinking Large Quantities of Liquid When Eating

For the most part, drink fluids between meals. Large quantities of fluids dilute and decrease the effectiveness of digestive enzymes and gastric juices, such as hydrochloric acid and pepsin, which your body secretes to break down protein. Cold liquids are especially problematic. They decrease the temperature of the cells of the stomach lining and slow down their metabolism, further compromising digestion. Instead of drinking during meals, have a glass or two of water about ten minutes beforehand.

Layer Your Food

As mentioned above, certain foods, particularly proteins and fats, spend more time in the stomach, whereas fruit needs very little time in the stomach and most carbohydrates fall somewhere in between. To help ease digestion, you could layer your food at a meal, eating foods that spend the least time in the stomach first and finishing with foods that spend the longest time in the stomach. The amount of time foods spend in the stomach also varies with quantities and overall stomach function, but here are typical times:

- Water: 5 minutes
- Water-rich fruit (such as melons): 5 minutes
- Dense fruit (such as bananas, dates, and figs): 20 minutes
- Water-rich vegetables and leafy greens: 30 to 45 minutes
- Grains and starchy vegetables: 45 to 60 minutes
- Legumes: 60 to 90 minutes
- Fats: 90 to 120 minutes

Note that fats slow down stomach emptying the most and, when combined with other foods, will prolong the time they spend in the stomach.

Avoid Overeating

Eat slowly and stop eating before you feel full. Be aware that it takes a while (about twenty minutes) for the brain to receive the signal that the stomach is full, so if you eat until you feel full, you're likely to overeat. Excessive food won't be fully broken down and absorbed, and it places a strain on the digestive system. This helps explain why overeating typically leads to loss of physical energy. There are other downsides to overeating. Studies of groups of people who have the greatest longevity find that they typically eat 50 percent fewer calories than typical North Americans. Studies have also shown a decrease in biological age in people who adopt a frugal eating style (reduced calories). Of course, when eating frugally it's important to eat only the freshest, most nutrient-dense foods.

Consider Digestive Aids

As you allow your digestive system to heal by making better food choices and paying attention to the digestive process, you may also want to take digestive aids, at least temporarily. These products contain ingredients that simulate digestive secretions and assist in the breakdown of food. You can usually find them in the supplements aisle at natural food stores.

Fast at Least Fourteen Hours per Day

Taking a long break from eating gives your digestive system a rest, builds digestive fire, and allows available energy to be used for building and repairing cells and detoxification, rather than digestion. Try to finish eating about three hours before retiring for bed and wait until you're hungry in the morning before you eat. Break your fast with foods that are easy to digest, such as fruit or a smoothie. If you're still hungry, perhaps have cooked whole grains such as brown rice, oats, or quinoa.

Create a Beautiful Setting

Use candles, flowers, attractive table settings, and other special touches to enhance the atmosphere. This beauty celebrates the sacredness of mealtime and will help you slow down and appreciate the food. A pleasing atmosphere helps your heart open and allows your being to receive what it needs and let go of what it doesn't need. In this setting, it becomes easier to make health-supporting food choices and enjoy the benefits of good digestion.

Bless Your Food

When you sit down with your meal in front of you, take a breath and make space for a blessing to arise. If this is an unfamiliar practice, just see what comes. In silence, and with beautiful nourishing food in front of you, an outpouring of gratitude is natural. In this space, you may see and feel the earth, rain, sun, and all of nature, as well as the many people who somehow were a part of bringing this food to your table. If it feels right to you, say a prayer, either from memory or inspired by the moment. If you're sharing your meal, hold hands as you offer your blessing.

Detoxification

In an ideal world, the body would remove toxins on an ongoing basis and would remain in perfect working order. Unfortunately, our bodies are often repositories for toxins in many forms: chemicals, drugs, food residues, heavy metals, fat, diseased and cancerous cells, tumors, cysts and fibroids, hardened arteries, kidney stones and gallstones, and more. Many diseases are caused by this buildup of toxicity in the system. The physical symptoms of these illnesses occur at the weakest link in the body, which varies from person to person. Two people with the same lifestyle might develop different diseases depending on which internal organs are most vulnerable. Another important factor is where people hold tension and unexpressed emotional energy. (For a list of signs and symptoms, see the sidebar on page 26.)

Happily, if you consistently consume a high-quality, whole-foods, plant-based diet, your body can more effectively cleanse itself and detoxify. To understand why, it's helpful to understand that there are six distinct stages to the processing of food by the body: intake, digestion, distribution, utilization, detoxification, and elimination.

For example, when you eat an apple, you bite into it, chew it, and swallow it (intake). Then the digestive system secretes enzymes and digestive fluids to break it down into smaller components so that its nutrients can be absorbed through the wall of the small intestine (digestion). Once in the bloodstream, vitamins, minerals, amino acids, essential fatty acids, and sugars are directed to the liver, which either sends them into storage or makes them available for immediate use for energy, growth, or repair (distribution and utilization). If the apple contained pesticides, preservatives, or other toxins, ideally the liver would pull them out of circulation to protect the body (detoxification). Indigestible fiber passes through the entire length of the small and large intestine to be eliminated with a bowel movement the next day (elimination). Simple enough.

Why Toxins Build Up in the System

Various factors can cause toxins to build up in your body. Although the colon, kidneys, liver, lymphatic system, and skin all help process and eliminate toxins, many people take in or are exposed to more toxins than these organs of detoxification and elimination can handle. Dietary toxins include pesticides, chemicals, preservatives, and denatured foods, such as processed oils. Another factor is eating foods that are difficult to digest, such as fried foods, meat, poor-quality dairy products, refined flour, and allergenic foods. Processing these foods fatigues the digestive organs and overloads detoxification systems.

Another issue is eating too much, too often, or both. This requires the body to spend too much time and energy on digestion, sapping resources of time and energy needed for elimination and detoxification. In addition, eating food that's beyond the body's digestive capacity, whether due to amount or quality, may lead to putrefaction of undigested food in the digestive tract, adding to the toxic burden. When these patterns are repeated for years on end, the abuse fatigues the organs of digestion and elimination, impairing their general ability to perform the tasks necessary for digestion, distribution, utilization, detoxification, and elimination.

Supporting the Body's Natural Rhythms

The body is naturally geared toward accomplishing various phases of food processing at certain times of the day. You can aid it in supporting your health by working with these natural rhythms:

- The best time for intake and digestion is between noon and 8 p.m., so take in most of your calories and your heartiest meals during this time.
- The optimal time for distribution and utilization is between 8 p.m. and 4 a.m. Avoid eating during this time.
- The best time for detoxification and elimination is between 4 a.m. and noon. Minimize eating during this time, and stick to simpler foods. Many people have a difficult time with this, because they've been programmed to believe that breakfast is the most important meal of the day. Notice if you're truly hungry in the morning. If you are hungry, try lighter foods like fruit and smoothies for your first meal of the day. Also notice how you feel when and after you eat.

Minimizing the Need for Detoxification

You can minimize your body's toxic load by eating the highest-quality, freshest foods possible. Your diet should be composed of 70 to 80 percent vegetables (especially leafy greens), fruits, sprouts, and herbs. These are the least congesting, most cleansing foods. (Congesting foods are those that tend to be hard to digest and build up in the body in the form of intestinal plaque, toxic residue in the liver and other organs, cysts, tumors and other growths, inflammation, and excess body fat.) Another 20 to 30 percent of your diet should consist of whole grains, legumes, starchy vegetables, nuts, and seeds. They supply nutrients needed for the production and regeneration of cells but are moderately congesting if eaten in excess.

It's equally important to eliminate the most congesting substances: dairy products, eggs, fried foods, hydrogenated fats, meat in general (and particularly organ meats), refined flour, sugar, processed and refined foods in general, and any foods you're sensitive or allergic to. The most common food sensitivities are to sugar, caffeine, wheat, gluten, dairy, soy, peanuts, nuts, corn, and citrus. And, though perhaps it goes without saying, be sure to follow the guidelines for good digestion on pages 19 to 25.

Where Toxins Come From

We are exposed to toxins from many sources. Toxins fall into two primary categories: exogenous and endogenous.

Exogenous toxins come from outside of the body. They enter through the mouth (from beverages, foods, medications, and so on), the skin (from body care products, cosmetics, detergent residues, fabrics, water, and so on), and the lungs (from the air and smoke). Specific examples of dietary exogenous toxins include processed foods, refined oils, white sugar, white flour, and so on, and also food additives and preservatives. Other key exogenous toxins include air pollution, household cleaners, cosmetics and beauty products, mercury from amalgam fillings, outgassing from materials used in construction and furnishings, plastics, and radiation.

Endogenous toxins come from within the body. They are typically by-products of metabolic processes, particularly digestion. Examples include acidity from acid-forming foods, cellular wastes, putrefying food residues, and waste products of parasitic microorganisms, including fungi and candida. Sometimes toxins are less concrete. Because emotions and thoughts can activate the stress response, they can lead to the creation of endogenous toxins. Therefore, toxins also include lifestyle factors such as unmanaged stress, overworking, noise pollution, information overload from the media (television, newspapers, radio, the Internet), repressed emotions, lack of emotional balance, and false and damaging beliefs about yourself, others, or the world at large.

Notice that almost all of these sources of toxins are things that are within your power to control. You can avoid many of them or make changes to reduce your exposure.

Signs and Symptoms of Toxicity

Here are some commons signs and symptoms that may indicate that your body is struggling with an excessive toxic burden:

Aches and pains

arthritis
fibromyalgia
gout
low back pain
stiff muscles and joints

Addictions

alcohol
caffeine
drugs
nicotine
sugar

Allergies

congestion
itchy eyes
itchy skin
sinus inflammation

Blood sugar imbalances

adult-onset diabetes (type 2)
childhood diabetes (type 1)
hypoglycemia

Bone and joint diseases

arthritis
osteoporosis
rheumatoid arthritis

Brain diseases

Alzheimer's disease
dementia
Parkinson's disease

Cardiovascular disease

atherosclerosis
heart disease
hypertension
stroke

Digestive issues

acid reflux
bloating
coated tongue
constipation
gas
hiatal hernia
nausea

Digestive system diseases

colitis
Crohn's disease
diverticulitis
gallstones
irritable bowel syndrome

Emotional instability

anxiety
depression
mood swings

Fatigue

insomnia
not feeling rested in the morning

Female cycle disturbances

cysts
fibroids
irregular periods
menopausal symptoms
painful periods
premenstrual syndrome

Headaches

migraine headaches
sinus headaches
tension headaches

Immune-system-related diseases

AIDS
cancer
lupus
multiple sclerosis

Infections

bacterial infection
fungal infection
parasitic infection
viral infection

Negative mind patterns

close-mindedness
inability to concentrate
negative thoughts
overactive mind

Respiratory disturbances

asthma
bronchitis
coughing
emphysema
wheezing

Skin issues

acne
boils
dryness
eczema
eye circles and bags
psoriasis

Weight imbalances

overweight
underweight

CHAPTER 3

Transformation and Balance

Soon after I began consciously improving my health through nutrition and lifestyle and teaching others to do the same, I became fascinated with the process of human change. Originally, I focused my efforts on educating people about health-supportive choices, but I found that one of the biggest challenges people faced was sorting through the overwhelming amount of health information they could access. I now feel that what we most need is a way to access our inner wisdom, which can provide the clearest guidance in all aspects of life—not least of which is how to care for the body. It's certainly helpful when information confirms the practices we're drawn to and encouraging when health practitioners help us clarify something we've been struggling with. Yet I've noticed that, with all the information that's available these days, many people, including health practitioners, are challenged to the point of frustration with having to consistently make choices that are life- and health-supporting, and with finding the time to implement these choices. Evidently, good intentions are not enough.

Dietary Changes and Emotional Detoxification

In general, when people embark on a path toward more nutritious eating, they understand the concept of physical detoxification. When you eat a diet that's clean, nutrient dense, and easy to digest, you're giving your body everything it needs to access its innate ability to heal itself. However, most of us aren't prepared for the emotional detoxification that occurs as a result of transitioning to a whole-foods plant-based diet.

Emotional Eating

Why does this happen? Simply put, most people's food choices are driven by emotions, not physical need. When we choose caffeinated beverages, pastries, sweets, or foods that are salty or rich (including so-called nutritious versions of these foods), these choices are governed less by how alive and well we think we'll feel after eating them and more by the momentary satisfaction they seem to offer. Food is probably the most common and most socially accepted way of soothing emotions. Emotional eating begins early in childhood when our caregivers offer us food rather than encouraging us to express our feelings. We carry this pattern into adulthood and continue to look to food for comfort and distraction from emotions or use eating to repress and numb undesired emotional experiences.

Unfortunately, most people don't find a healthful diet all that comforting. Refined foods provide a rush of energy that brings temporary pleasure and soothing. You can try to replace typical comfort foods with more healthful versions, for example, by baking with whole-grain flours, cold-pressed oils, and natural sweeteners. However, resorting to even these improved versions too often won't support health in the long run. Ultimately, you have to face the difficult emotions. This is the path to discovering the suppressed emotions and habitual negative energy patterns that are the root cause of poor lifestyle choices and, often, poor health.

Activation of Old Emotions

Approaching this issue from another angle, all foods are made up of energy with varying levels of vibration. Foods that are processed, that contain chemicals or elements of human or animal suffering, or that damage the planet during their production have a lower vibration. Those with the highest vibrations are unprocessed, raw, whole, organic, locally grown, and prepared with love and gratitude. If, like most people in Western cultures, you're accustomed to eating low-vibration foods, when you switch to a diet of high-vibration, plant-based whole foods, you'll undergo not only physical detoxification, but emotional detoxification as well.

Why? Emotions also have varying levels of energy vibration. We store emotional imprints in our bodies from the multitude of experiences we've had since birth, particularly those emotional memories that weren't completely processed at the time of the experience because we weren't encouraged to express ourselves, or because we felt shame around the experience, or because the adults around us didn't have the capacity to be present for us during those challenging times. The emotional imprints you've absorbed on your journey can be seen and felt by intuitive people as dense pockets of energy in your energy field. When you adopt a higher-vibration diet, the resulting lightening in the body allows dense, often painful emotions to rise to the surface of your awareness. Yet at the same time, you are no longer relying on many or most of your former food-based emotional crutches.

In this situation, many people find themselves sliding back toward unhealthful food choices in a subconscious effort to repress old emotions that have been reactivated. Many of my clients report that after adopting a more nutritious diet and initially experiencing a high of increased energy and decreased symptoms, they begin to struggle with challenging emotions, such as anger, anxiety, fear, and sadness. Simultaneously, they begin to struggle with the dietary changes that at first seemed so effortless.

A Process of Self-Discovery

I feel that this process of emotional detoxification is actually one of the greatest gifts of a healthful diet. However, people need to be aware that this will probably occur and find ways to allow old emotions to move through them and out of them. It's a beautiful process to unearth old emotions, to allow them to dance their way out of your system and let them go, revealing ever more of your shining, authentic beauty. Yet it does take time to develop the grounding, spiritual connection and emotional stamina necessary to staying balanced while eating a very high-vibration diet.

In addition, consuming a whole-foods, plant-based diet can make you far more sensitive to surrounding energies. If you live in the city, this can present a greater challenge. It takes time to strengthen your energy field through spiritual practice, awareness, counseling, or the help of holistic practitioners so that you can withstand the effects of artificial lighting, traffic, noise, crowding, pollution, and other challenging aspects of urban life.

When I work with clients, I recommend that they quit eating processed foods, reduce the amount of animal products they eat, and increase their consumption of whole plant foods, starting with about 30 percent raw foods. I also recommend daily meditation and an ongoing spiritual practice, which serves as a foundation for maintaining a strong connection with the soul—the true guide in navigating emotional energy. I encourage clients to let their level of balance and joy be the gauge for when to make changes in food and lifestyle choices. While it is helpful to follow guidelines for maintaining health, rigid rules tend to be detrimental.

Rather than imposing food choices on yourself or your family, let the process be fluid and joyful. If you're willing to listen, your body will tell you when to decrease or cut out animal products, when to increase your consumption of raw foods, and so on. For example, you may need more cooked or dense food when you're going through a period of particularly accelerated spiritual growth, which always includes letting go of emotions. You also need to trust the ability of your children, partner, and other loved ones to choose appropriate, health-supporting foods for themselves. Their physical, emotional, and spiritual needs are undoubtedly different from yours.

Making Peace with Your Food Choices

When we are clear, we have direct access to our intuition about what is best for our individual health—something that cannot be adequately expressed in books. This knowledge is imprinted in the very cells that make up our bodies. We all have access to this wisdom. However, most if not all of our food choices are governed by deeply ingrained patterns influenced or even dictated by social and family messages and maintained subconsciously. For the most part, these patterns are driven by emotions and anchored in false beliefs.

While I share many practical ideas, recipes, how-tos, and recommendations in this book, I'm well aware that reading those suggestions won't be enough to create lasting change, no matter how helpful or even inspiring they may be. How many of us have committed to making better choices only to find ourselves reverting to old habits later, sometimes as soon as the next meal? I mention this not to create shame or guilt, but to help shed light on the fact that discipline and high ideals are not enough; after all, everyone has these tendencies. In fact, discipline and high ideals sometimes prevent us from listening to the quiet inner guidance the body itself provides.

You may be wondering how you can make peace with your food choices or how you can learn to trust your body. You may be wondering how you can find the time in already busy days for preparing nutritious food or how you can let go of the frustration you feel with your family's unwillingness to eat more healthfully.

Perhaps the answers to some of these questions lie in changing your perspective. One of the primary teachings of the Buddha is that all suffering stems from false beliefs. It could be profoundly helpful to inquire into your beliefs about food—to question them and assess them honestly. Here are some of the common limiting beliefs I hear from students and clients:

I Need to Find the Perfect Diet

There is no perfect diet. The diet that works well for one person may not be suitable for another. The diet that worked for you last year may not work for you now. Eventually, after trying to adhere to a series of recommended diets (and some people seem to have quite literally tried them all), you have no choice but to give up trying to be perfect. Let go of rigid mind-made rules and instead humbly get still, listen to your body, and trust.

I Don't Know How to Listen to My Body

You may have ignored your body for a long time, but you can start to open the doors of communication right now. This very moment, turn your awareness inward. What do you feel? Where is there tension in your body? How are you breathing? Observe without judging or rationalizing. Just listen openly. When you're ready to choose your next meal, stop and take a moment to ask your body what it needs. Get a sense of whether you are truly hungry or not. Notice whether you need something heavy and dense, something light and fresh, something sweet, or something savory. Even if you don't feel you're receiving much information from your body at first, just keep being open.

I Can't Control My Cravings

While it's true that you can't control your cravings, you can explore them and be open to what they're teaching you. When you crave food that you know won't make you feel good after you eat it, take a moment to feel where the need is coming from in your body. Be curious about what you're feeling and do your best to make friends with the feeling. Since the feeling is driving the craving, the craving will dissipate on its own once the feeling is acknowledged and integrated. Here's an example from my own experience. Years ago I got into the habit of having toast with butter and honey in the evening. When I decided to tune in to what I was feeling, I noticed that when the craving came I felt a sense of hollowness in my arms and across my chest. It felt like loneliness. I went ahead and, without distractions, ate the toast. I noticed that although it tasted good in the moment, the feeling of hollowness or loneliness remained unchanged. Satisfying my craving wasn't making a dent in the true issue. After that, I started to allow the feeling of loneliness into my meditations, and over time it has become lighter, much less predominant, and less scary.

I Don't Have the Time to Prepare Healthful Foods

The truth is, we all find time to do the things that are important to us. If you're not finding time to shop for and prepare nutritious food at this point, that's perfectly fine. But you need to be honest and acknowledge that you do have the time. It need not take more than five minutes to make a smoothie, ten minutes to put together a hearty salad, or twenty minutes to make a satisfying soup that can be the center of several good meals. Most people spend quite a few hours watching television, talking on the phone, surfing the Internet, shopping for unnecessary items, and so forth. Also realize that eating health-promoting food will actually give you more time; as your health improves, you'll have more energy, enthusiasm, and focus, not to mention less need to distract yourself with television, the Internet, and shopping!

I'm Not a Good Cook

Anyone can learn how to prepare tasty food. Follow recipes precisely (especially at first), take some cooking classes, seek advice and guidance from like-minded friends, and allow some time in your schedule for activities related to food preparation.

My Family Doesn't Like Nutritious Food

Do your family members have to change their habits, or is this your expectation? Do others need to eat the same way you do, or is this simply your ideal? How would you feel if someone pressured you to make changes you weren't ready for? If you relax around your expectations of others, focus on preparing tasty and wholesome food, and joyfully share your creations with your friends and family, you're likely to find that they'll come along in their own time. Even if they don't, you'll probably find that things go more smoothly when you remove yourself from other people's business—and their food choices are their business. Instead, focus on your own business: your food choices.

I believe the most important quality in this health-seeking journey is sincerity. When you're sincere, you'll stay on the path of your unique journey. You'll recognize your power over false beliefs about yourself and your body and be open to exercising that power, whether those false beliefs are characterized by commonly held views of health and nutrition, a need for approval from outsiders, a sense of powerlessness over addictions, or inauthentic values. When you reconnect to an inner power that is rooted in the ground of your true nature, you'll find an unlimited source of self-knowledge and the ability to make life-supportive choices with confidence.

Practical Advice on Transitioning to a Healthier Household

While the food philosophies I've shared are important—foundational, really—bringing these concepts into your day-to-day life is a concrete undertaking. So let's take a look at practical approaches that may be helpful.

Changing a family's routines can be hard. Ease the transition by engaging everyone in the decision-making process. Have a family meeting. Discuss the changes you'd like to make and explain why they're important to you. Ask for everybody's input, then work together to arrive at a peaceful compromise and develop a strategy for implementing it.

When you're transitioning to a new way of cooking and eating, it's helpful to plan menus for about a week in advance. Choose foods and recipes that are relatively familiar to your family and keep your menus simple at first. Go through the recipes you plan to cook and make a shopping list of everything you'll need. Somewhere in your kitchen, keep a running list of groceries you need to purchase, and be sure to add to it anytime you run out of staple items. At first you may find that your grocery lists are longer than you're accustomed to as you stock up on the ingredients necessary for whole-foods cooking. Rest assured that as the weeks pass, you'll be buying fewer new items and spending less.

You'll probably find that your improved eating habits initially require more time in food preparation. It does take more time to put together a typical meal using fresh, whole ingredients than it does to rely on processed, packaged foods. Convenience foods and fast-food restaurants have warped our expectations about the time required to prepare food. My grandmother, a farmer's wife with twelve children living in eastern Quebec, used to spend most of her waking hours growing, preparing, and preserving food. If she wasn't planting or harvesting, she was plucking a chicken, making bread, or canning for the winter. There were always three big meals to make every day, followed by cleanup and preparations for the next meal. Nowadays, many of us have filled our days with so much activity that we find it stressful to set aside a half hour to prepare the occasional meal.

As you begin to value healthful, whole-foods meals for the profound life-enhancing qualities they have, you will naturally begin to make time for preparing them. Plus, once you discover new stores, fill your cupboards with staples, acquire a repertoire of favorite quick recipes, and adjust to your new routine, the amount of time you need to spend in the kitchen will decrease.

Personally, I spend anywhere from forty-five to ninety minutes a day in the kitchen, including preparation and cleanup. Once a week I devote a longer period of time to organizing, cleaning out my refrigerator, dehydrating or otherwise preserving foods, and making things in advance to speed preparation time in the days ahead. Here are some tips that I've found helpful. I hope they help you as well:

- Set aside the time that you need to prepare meals.

- Buy good-quality appliances, utensils, and cookware to make your job easier.

- Keep your meals simple.

- If you're new to whole-foods cuisine, follow recipes closely and carefully the first time you prepare a dish. As you become more comfortable with ingredients and techniques, you can be more creative and use recipes for inspiration rather than as a rigid structure.

- Do as much advance preparation as possible, especially if you get home from work or school close to dinnertime.

- Keep your kitchen stocked with fresh vegetables, fruits, grains, dried and canned legumes, seeds, nuts, crackers, whole-grain breads, pastas, and jarred sauces. These can provide the foundation for all sorts of nutritious meals.

- Organize your kitchen and keep it simple, clean, and inviting. Put similar items in the same cupboards. Keep dried fruits, grains, flours, dried legumes, seeds, and nuts in labeled glass jars to ensure freshness and make them easy to find. If you have room in your refrigerator or freezer, cold storage of nuts and flours will extend freshness.

- Always have a big pot of hearty soup at hand. Most soups can be stored in the refrigerator for up to three days. Soup is an ideal nutritious snack, or add a salad and you have a great lunch or easy dinner. For packed lunches, put some hot soup in a thermos for a warm meal away from home.

- Always have at least one spread or filling on hand for wraps, sandwiches, or pita pockets. Baba ganoush, grilled vegetables, guacamole, hummus, and tofu salad all come in handy here.

- It may be tempting to make double batches of certain recipes for convenience sake, and if time is a limiting factor, by all means do so. However, be aware that freshly made food is at its peak in terms of flavor, texture, and nutrition. Still, leftovers of healthful and lovingly prepared food are probably a better bet than most convenience foods. Just be sure to store leftovers in a sealed container in the refrigerator or freezer. Most foods will keep for three days.

- Children need not be a distraction from cooking. They can sit at the kitchen table and play or do homework or crafts. They can also help out with some of the food preparation.

- Ask your family to be open to trying new dishes, but don't expect them to be delighted with every new concoction you create, especially at first. With time they may come to like dishes they initially resisted. That's what I've found with my children.

- Be patient with yourself and your family. As with all changes, shifting one's diet can still be stressful, even if it's for the best. Stay motivated by connecting with friends who share your interest in health, by taking cooking classes, and by consulting books that reflect and support your new dietary direction.

About Children and Food

It's natural to want your children to eat the most healthful diet possible. However, do remember that we can't make others do anything (even though we really do try to control our children!). However, we do have choices about our own actions, and these are the most important influences on our children. If your children see you making healthful choices and sincerely enjoying real food, you'll provide a positive example upon which they can model their own attitudes regarding their bodies and food. If, on the other hand, mealtime is fraught with struggles and arguments, this can result in ongoing power struggles, emotional eating, and poor food choices. Fortunately, this negativity can be undone with willingness and love.

Take a look at your own attitudes regarding healthful eating. It's likely that your children will reflect back to you any unresolved issues you have. If you're feeling guilty about the treat you had last night, you may find yourself nagging your children about the junk they're eating today. If you get angry at your children for complaining about a meal, maybe you're less than thrilled with the food you've been preparing lately. There's a story about a woman who took her daughter to Gandhi and asked him to tell her daughter to stop eating so much sugar. Gandhi told them to come back the next week. When they arrived, Gandhi told the daughter to stop eating sugar. The mother asked why he didn't tell her that the previous week. Gandhi replied that he had to stop eating sugar himself first.

Here are some pointers that I hope will be helpful for you and your children. Apply those that feel most natural for now, and most of all, be sure to keep mealtimes enjoyable:

- Let go of control. Trust that children will naturally make good choices over time if they're given the freedom to make their own selections and experience the consequences.
- Get children involved with meal planning and preparation. Ask them what dishes they like, then modify those by using whole-food ingredients and adding more vegetables little by little. Likewise, you can modify recipes by substituting vegetables they like for those they think they don't care for.
- Bring children along when shopping and let them make choices about what to purchase.
- Pile appealing fresh fruits in baskets in a prominent place in the kitchen. Another option for snacks is sliced fruits and vegetables with nut butters or dips.
- If your children turn up their noses at all vegetables, try seasoning the vegetables with a little sea salt, cold-pressed oil, or Cheesy Sauce (page 115).

- Find nutritious alternatives to your children's favorite foods. Examples include sparkling juice instead of carbonated beverages, cereal bars or granola bars instead of candy, and homemade comfort foods, such as Vegan Macaroni and Cheese with Broccoli (page 138), Root Fries (page 160), and Vegetable Calzones (page 141).

- Hearty soups are a great way to serve legumes and vegetables to children, and they can be served at lunch or dinner and even as a snack.

- Consider not keeping processed food in the house. In my experience, there are plenty of opportunities to partake of poor-quality offerings outside the house at friends' homes and at restaurants.

- When eating out, choose restaurants with nutritious choices. Children get mixed messages when whole foods are served at home but the family opts for fast food when eating out. Fortunately, increasing numbers of restaurants are serving healthful foods these days thanks to consumer demand.

- Talk to your children about how food can affect their bodies, minds, and emotions, but do your best to steer clear of lecturing.

- If your children are feeling tired or sick after eating junk food, gently help them to draw the connection.

- Make wholesome eating a priority in your family's life. This means making time to shop for and prepare high-quality food. This also applies to when and how you eat. Try to have at least one meal together as a family every day.

Embrace the Possibilities

At the core of your being, you hold the potential to be healthy in all senses of the word, to be free of disease, and even to reverse disease. When you embrace these possibilities, you'll find that all sorts of new information and insights will come into your life to support you along the way—perhaps from books or workshops, or even from chance encounters. Let the process be fluid, effortless, and joyful.

Packed Lunch Suggestions

The suggestions below are oriented toward kids' school lunches. However, all are portable, delicious, and nutritious, and who says adults can't enjoy them as well? Packed lunches are definitely an enlightened eating choice because they allow you to ensure that all of the foods are healthful and nutritious; plus, they're generally more economical than the alternatives. Because of the various concerns about plastic, including its toxicity, it's best to package lunch items in reusable glass or stainless steel containers. When packing lunches, choose from the following and aim for variety in any given lunch and from day to day:

- **Fruit:** apple, berries, grapes, mango, melon, pear, pineapple, and so on
- **Dried fruit:** apricots, cranberries, dates, figs, raisins, and so on, or fruit leathers
- **Nuts and seeds:** almonds, cashews, pecans, walnuts, and so on (may not be allowed at some schools)
- **Raw veggies:** carrot, celery, cherry tomatoes, cucumber, red bell pepper, and so on
- **Soups** (packed in a thermos)
- **Smoothies** (packed in a thermos)
- **Salads:** Cabbage Salad with Apple, Pecans, and Raisins (page 101), Five-Bean Salad (page 107), Rice and Bean Salad with Cashews (page 110), a green salad with homemade dressing, and so on
- **Sandwiches and wraps:** Heavenly Hummus (page 70) and vegetables in a whole-grain wrap, Vegetable Calzones (page 141), and so on
- **Leftovers**

General Recommendations for Health

In these introductory chapters, I've given you a number of suggestions on diet and lifestyle that can help you elevate your health and well-being to a higher level. Here's a brief recap of key points for easy reference.

MEALS

- Start your day with a glass or two of pure water.
- Wait to eat breakfast until you're hungry, and then break your fast with as much fruit as you like. Consider a fruit salad, such as Harvest Fruit Salad (page 42). If you need something warming, try Whole-Grain Porridge with Berries and Almond Milk (page 43).
- If you have fresh fruit for breakfast, follow up with a smoothie (see pages 56 to 60). If you need to head out to start your day, pack it in a glass jar and take it with you.
- For lunch, have a hearty salad meal (see Suggestions, p. 37). There are many suitable recipes in this book (for example, Asian Quinoa and Tofu Salad, page 109; Soba Noodle Salad with Baby Bok Choy, page 105; Cabbage Salad with Apple, Pecans, and Raisins, page 101; or Kale-Avocado Salad, page 99). Add a vegetable soup, if desired, or whole-grain crackers or bread with a spread or dip.
- If you want a snack in the midafternoon or before dinner, make some fresh juice (see pages 61 to 64).
- For dinner, have a delicious meal of vegetables, whole grains, and legumes.
- Change things up by making lunch your main meal and enjoying a hearty salad for dinner.

MOVEMENT

- Start with whatever exercise you can do and gradually increase the length and intensity as it feels right.

- Incorporate some movement every day, either all at one time or interspersed throughout the day.
- Three to five times per week, practice yoga, dance, or any holistic movement form, such as tai chi or qi gong, to promote body awareness, strength, flexibility, conscious breathing, balance, and coordination.
- Do some sort of aerobic exercise—walking, dancing, rollerblading, swimming, running, or any activity that elevates the heart rate—four to six times per week for at least twenty minutes per session.
- Incorporate outdoor activities daily, such as gardening or walking, or take traditionally indoor activities outdoors, such as eating or meditation.

LIFESTYLE

- Breathe fresh air. If outdoor air quality is good, be active outdoors, and when you're indoors, open windows whenever feasible. If indoor air quality is an issue, use an air filtration system in your home or at least grow some houseplants.
- Drink pure water. Make sure your drinking water is purified, alkaline, and mineralized. It's also a good idea to bathe in pure water, so consider installing a shower filter.
- Take in some sunshine. Enjoy the gentle early morning sun whenever possible.
- Get enough rest. Go to bed at a reasonably early hour and sleep a sufficient amount of time to feel rested. If you're inclined, and time permits, take a short nap in the afternoon.
- Take some unscheduled time for yourself every day.
- Clean up your home environment. Simplify and unclutter. Be sure to use natural, nontoxic products for cleaning.
- Use natural, nontoxic body care products.

TEND TO MIND AND SPIRIT

- Be aware of how you feel—physically, mentally, and emotionally—before, while, and after you eat. This will provide important information to guide you in making more health-supporting food choices.

- Turn awareness toward areas of discomfort in your body with openness and receptivity and notice any insights that arise.

- Feed your mind and spirit with inspirational readings, beautiful music, and uplifting art, movies, and plays.

- Explore and express your natural gifts and abilities.

- Take care of your closest relationships. Resolve conflicts through personal work and introspection, spiritual practice, and counseling.

- Set aside time for silence every day. Sitting in the stillness of your body is a powerful way to access peace. Open up to that authentic place that exists beyond your changing body, beliefs, thoughts, emotions, and circumstances.

Salad Meal Suggestions

Choose from the following ingredients to make endless variations on hearty salad meals. I suggest using generous amounts of leafy greens for their healthful properties and adding other ingredients depending on your preferences and what's in season. To ensure that your salad is substantial enough to serve as a meal, you'll probably want to include legumes, grains, noodles, nuts, or seeds.

- **Greens:** arugula, baby salad greens, green or red leaf lettuce, romaine lettuce, and so on

- **Sprouts:** alfalfa, broccoli, clover, lentil, mung bean, radish, sunflower, and other varieties of sprouts

- **Grated root vegetables:** beets, carrots, daikon radish

- **Classic salad vegetables:** bell peppers, cucumbers, tomatoes

- **Other vegetables:** asparagus, corn, fennel, green or red cabbage, peas

- **Cooked legumes:** baked tofu, black beans, chickpeas, kidney beans, and so on

- **Cooked grains:** brown rice, millet, quinoa, and so on

- **Cooked noodles:** brown rice noodles, buckwheat soba noodles, and so on

- **Nuts or seeds**

- **Green or red onions**

- **Avocado or olives**

- **Fermented or pickled vegetables**

- **Fresh herbs:** basil, chives, cilantro, oregano, tarragon, thyme, and so on

- **Salad dressing** (see pages 116 to 121)

As an ancient Chinese saying advises, "Do not use force to conquer the universe, for this would only cause resistance. Force is followed by a loss of strength." If you apply too much effort on your path to health, you'll become tired and disillusioned. From my experience, the most lasting changes arise from inspiration. A light goes on inside you that simply reveals, "It's time." You find yourself ready for a new shift, a new addition to your health-supporting practices. Perhaps you'll start juicing, begin to practice meditation, commit to an exercise program, or give up meat. Whatever it may be, the universe will gracefully meet you to support your ongoing unfolding.

CHAPTER 4

Breakfast Dishes and Quick Breads

What makes this fruit salad special is an abundance of juice. In fact, it's so juicy it could be called a fruit soup. Whatever you call it, it's a delicious way to break your fast in the morning. Although it's best to serve this salad as soon as it's made, if you aren't hungry first thing in the morning you can put it in a glass jar and take it with you to enjoy later.

SUMMER fruit salad

MAKES 4 SERVINGS

4 peaches with peel, diced

1 cup blueberries

1 cup pitted cherries

2 cups unsweetened apple juice

1. Put the peaches, blueberries, and cherries in a medium bowl and stir gently to combine.

2. Gently stir in the apple juice.

The perfect season to have this juicy breakfast is spring, when local fruits may be unavailable and tropical fruits are at their best.

tropical FRUIT SALAD

MAKES 4 SERVINGS

2 mangoes, diced (see note)

2 bananas, sliced

2 cups diced fresh pineapple

2 cups freshly squeezed orange juice (about 4 oranges)

¼ cup unsweetened shredded dried coconut (optional)

1. Put the mangoes, bananas, and pineapple in a medium bowl and stir gently to combine.

2. Gently stir in the orange juice and the optional coconut. Serve immediately.

NOTE: To dice mangoes, simply slice the two "cheeks" off the narrow pit, score the flesh into small squares, and then turn the "cheeks" inside out. Voilà! The mango cubes will be easy to cut off. Enjoy any flesh remaining on the pit and inside of the peel—but you'll probably want to eat it over the kitchen sink!

This meal, which is beautiful in its simplicity, is a satisfying breakfast year-round. You could also enjoy it for a quick light lunch or dinner. The celery adds soluble fiber, which helps with regularity and blood sugar control.

HARVEST fruit salad

See photo facing page 18.

See photo facing page 18.

MAKES 2 SERVINGS

2 large or 4 small apples with peel, diced

4 to 6 stalks celery, halved lengthwise and sliced

12 raw walnut or pecan halves, broken into pieces

½ cup raisins, cranberries, or currants or chopped figs, apricots, or dates

2 tablespoons hempseeds (optional)

Juice of 2 oranges or 1 cup unsweetened apple juice

1. Put the apples, celery, walnuts, raisins, and optional hempseeds in a medium bowl and stir gently to combine.

2. Stir in the orange juice. Serve immediately.

This filling hot cereal makes good use of leftover cooked grains and also features a trick for making almond milk quickly.

whole-grain porridge WITH BERRIES AND ALMOND MILK

MAKES 2 SERVINGS

2 cups cooked rice, quinoa, or millet

2½ cups water

4 pitted soft dates

2 tablespoons raw almond butter

1 cup fresh or thawed frozen berries

¼ cup chopped walnuts or pecans

Unrefined cane sugar (optional)

1. Put the rice in a medium saucepan with 1 cup of the water. Cook over medium-low heat until warm, stirring occasionally. Add a little more water if necessary to prevent sticking.

2. Make almond milk by putting the dates, almond butter, and remaining 1½ cups of water in a blender and processing until smooth.

3. To serve, divide the rice between two bowls and top with the berries. Pour half of the almond milk over each serving, then sprinkle half of the walnuts over each. Sweeten with unrefined cane sugar if desired.

These nutrition-packed pancakes are made with some of nature's most health-promoting and protein-rich grains: buckwheat and quinoa. They are denser than traditional pancakes. Cook up a bunch of these and leave them in the fridge for the on-the-go members of your family—no need to reheat!

BLUEBERRY pancakes

MAKES 15 (4-INCH) PANCAKES

½ cup buckwheat groats, soaked in water for 4 to 8 hours (see notes)

½ cup quinoa, soaked in water for 4 to 8 hours

1⅓ cups water

1 cup fresh or thawed and drained frozen blueberries

1 cup old-fashioned rolled oats

6 pitted soft dates

⅓ cup hempseeds

2 tablespoons ground flaxseeds

1 tablespoon extra-virgin olive oil

1 teaspoon vanilla extract

¾ teaspoon baking powder

¾ teaspoon baking soda

Pinch salt

1. Drain and rinse the buckwheat and quinoa in a fine-mesh strainer. Transfer to a blender.

2. Add the water, blueberries, oats, dates, hempseeds, flaxseeds, oil, vanilla extract, baking powder, baking soda, and salt. Process until smooth. Let the batter sit for 5 minutes.

3. Lightly oil a large skillet with cold-pressed coconut oil and heat over medium-low heat.

4. Pour in batter to make three 3-inch circles. Cover and cook for 5 minutes (see notes).

5. Flip and cook the other side for 5 minutes, uncovered. Serve hot.

NOTES

- The buckwheat and quinoa can be soaked together.
- The pancakes must be cooked for 5 minutes per side; otherwise they'll be doughy inside. Plan to make them while you're doing other work in the kitchen so that you're not standing at the stove waiting, which might tempt you to turn them or serve them too soon.

This delicious egg-free version of a favorite breakfast food hits the spot on cold mornings. The French toast is baked in the oven rather than fried in a pan. Serve it with Scrambled Tofu (page 46) for a meal that will keep you going for hours.

VEGAN french toast

8 slices whole-grain bread

2 cups Homemade Almond Milk (page 52) or other nondairy milk

3 tablespoons maple syrup, plus more for serving

1 teaspoon ground cinnamon

1 teaspoon vanilla extract

Pinch salt

2 cups fresh or thawed frozen peach slices (optional)

1. Preheat the oven to 350 degrees F.

2. Lightly oil a nonstick baking sheet with cold-pressed coconut oil or extra-virgin olive oil.

3. Cut each slice of bread diagonally into 2 triangles.

4. Put the almond milk, maple syrup, cinnamon, vanilla extract, and salt in a large, shallow bowl and whisk to combine.

5. Dip the bread in the almond milk mixture until well saturated, then arrange the pieces in a single layer on the prepared baking sheet.

6. Bake for 12 minutes. Flip with a spatula and bake for 10 minutes longer, until browned and slightly crusty.

7. Serve hot, topped with the optional peaches and additional maple syrup.

In addition to being a delicious addition to a hearty breakfast, Scrambled Tofu can be served on toast for a quick and filling meal. Try spreading ketchup on the toast first or putting a slice of tomato atop the tofu.

scrambled TOFU

2 tablespoons extra-virgin olive oil

1 pound firm tofu

2 tablespoons nutritional yeast

1½ tablespoons reduced-sodium tamari

1 teaspoon ground turmeric

½ teaspoon salt

½ cup water

Ground pepper

1. Put the oil in a medium saucepan over medium heat.

2. Crumble the tofu into the saucepan. Add the nutritional yeast, tamari, turmeric, and salt and mash with a potato masher or a fork.

3. Add the water and cook for 10 minutes, stirring occasionally.

4. Season with pepper. Taste and add more nutritional yeast, tamari, salt, or pepper if desired.

Moist and sweet, this classic bread is made with wholesome ingredients. Serve it with Homemade Almond Milk (page 52) for breakfast or for an afternoon or evening treat.

BANANA bread

MAKES 1 LOAF (9 SERVINGS)

2¼ cups mashed ripe bananas (about 5 bananas)

6 tablespoons expeller-pressed sunflower oil or cold-pressed coconut oil, melted

6 tablespoons maple syrup

¼ cup Homemade Almond Milk (page 52) or other nondairy milk

2 cups spelt flour or whole wheat flour

1 teaspoon baking soda

1 teaspoon baking powder

½ teaspoon salt

¾ cup chopped walnuts or pecans

¾ cup vegan chocolate chips (optional)

1. Preheat the oven to 350 degrees F.
2. Lightly oil an 8-inch square baking pan or an 8½ x 4½-inch loaf pan.
3. Put the bananas, oil, maple syrup, and nondairy milk in a blender and process until smooth.
4. Put the flour, baking soda, baking powder, and salt in a large bowl and mix well.
5. Pour the banana mixture into the flour mixture. Stir to combine, using as few strokes as possible.
6. Gently stir in the walnuts and optional chocolate chips until evenly distributed.
7. Pour into the prepared pan and smooth the top with a rubber spatula.
8. Bake for 30 to 35 minutes, until a toothpick inserted in the center comes out clean.
9. Cool completely before slicing or storing. Wrapped tightly with plastic wrap or stored in a ziplock bag, Banana Bread will keep for 3 days at room temperature or for 1 month in the freezer.

These pleasing low-fat muffins, with a subtle hint of lemon zest, use applesauce and flaxseeds to replace eggs. Pack them in school or work lunches to satisfy cravings for less healthful choices.

APPLESAUCE muffins

MAKES 12 LARGE MUFFINS OR 24 MINI MUFFINS

1 cup applesauce

½ cup Homemade Almond Milk (page 52) or other nondairy milk

⅓ cup maple syrup

3 tablespoons expeller-pressed sunflower oil or extra-virgin olive oil

2 tablespoons ground flaxseeds

2 cups spelt flour or whole wheat flour

2 tablespoons grated lemon zest

1 teaspoon baking soda

½ teaspoon salt

½ teaspoon ground cinnamon

1 cup raisins

1. Preheat the oven to 375 degrees F.

2. Lightly oil one 12-cup muffin pan or two 12-cup mini muffin pans.

3. Put the applesauce, nondairy milk, maple syrup, oil, and flaxseeds in a medium bowl and mix well.

4. Put the flour, zest, baking soda, salt, and cinnamon in a large bowl and mix well.

5. Pour the applesauce mixture into the flour mixture and stir to combine, using as few strokes as possible. Add the raisins and stir gently until evenly distributed.

6. Spoon the batter into the prepared muffin cups, filling each about three-quarters full.

7. Bake for 20 to 25 minutes for large muffins or 12 to 15 minutes for mini muffins, until a toothpick inserted in the center of a muffin comes out clean.

8. Let the muffins cool for 5 minutes before removing them from the pan.

9. Cool completely before storing. Stored in sealed containers or ziplock bags, Applesauce Muffins will keep for 3 days at room temperature or for 1 month in the freezer.

These rich and tasty muffins prove once again that baked goods can easily be made with low-fat, wholesome ingredients.

pear-ginger MUFFINS

1¾ cups spelt flour or whole wheat flour

2 teaspoon ground cinnamon

2 teaspoon baking powder

¾ teaspoon baking soda

¾ cup Homemade Almond Milk (page 52) or other nondairy milk

½ cup applesauce

¼ cup maple syrup

¼ cup extra-virgin olive oil or expeller-pressed sunflower oil

2 teaspoons peeled and grated fresh ginger

½ teaspoon cider vinegar

2 ripe pears, peeled and diced

1. Preheat the oven to 375 degrees F.
2. Lightly oil one 12-cup muffin pan or two 12-cup mini muffin pans.
3. Put the flour, cinnamon, baking powder, and baking soda in a large bowl and mix well.
4. Put the nondairy milk, applesauce, maple syrup, oil, ginger, and vinegar in a blender and process until well combined.
5. Pour the applesauce mixture into the flour mixture. Stir to combine, using as few strokes as possible.
6. Gently stir in the pears until evenly distributed.
7. Spoon the batter into the prepared muffin cups, filling each about three-quarters full.
8. Bake for 20 to 25 minutes for large muffins or 12 to 15 minutes for mini muffins, until a toothpick inserted in the center of a muffin comes out clean.
9. Let the muffins cool for 5 minutes before removing them from the pan.
10. Cool completely before storing. Stored in sealed containers or ziplock bags, Pear-Ginger Muffins will keep for 3 days at room temperature or for 1 month in the freezer.

Contributed by permission of Ricki Heller, dietdessertndogs.com.

These hearty muffins have many admirable nutritional features: the phytonutrients of a whole orange; the minerals of blackstrap molasses, dates, and raisins; and the soluble and insoluble fiber of a variety of whole-food ingredients. They're great for breakfast, but so portable that you can take them with you for a nourishing snack at any time of day.

orange-oatmeal MUFFINS

See photo on facing page.

MAKES 12 LARGE MUFFINS OR 24 MINI MUFFINS

1⅓ cups spelt flour or whole wheat flour

1 cup old-fashioned rolled oats

1 tablespoon baking powder

1 teaspoon baking soda

⅓ cup raisins

⅓ cup chopped walnuts or other raw nuts

1 orange

½ cup pitted soft dates

½ cup **Homemade Almond Milk** (page 52) or other nondairy milk

¼ cup blackstrap molasses

3 tablespoons extra-virgin olive oil or cold-pressed coconut oil

2 tablespoons maple syrup

2 tablespoons finely ground flaxseeds

1. Preheat the oven to 375 degrees F.

2. Lightly oil one 12-cup standard muffin pan or two 12-cup mini muffin pans.

3. Put the flour, oats, baking powder, and baking soda in a large bowl and mix well. Add the raisins and walnuts and toss to coat.

4. Wash and dry the orange. Cut it into 8 pieces and remove any seeds. Put the pieces in a food processor (yes, the whole orange) and process until almost smooth. Add the dates and process until thick and smooth. Add the nondairy milk, molasses, oil, maple syrup, and flaxseeds and process until well combined.

5. Pour the orange mixture into the flour mixture. Stir to combine, using as few strokes as possible.

6. Spoon the batter into the prepared muffin cups, filling each about three-quarters full.

7. Bake for 20 to 25 minutes for large muffins or 12 to15 minutes for mini muffins, until a toothpick inserted in the center of a muffin comes out clean.

8. Let the muffins cool for 5 minutes before removing them from the pan.

9. Cool completely before storing. Stored in sealed containers or ziplock bags, Orange-Oatmeal Muffins will keep for 3 days at room temperature or for 1 month in the freezer.

Contributed by permission of Ricki Heller, dietdessertndogs.com.

Orange-Oatmeal Muffins, *facing page*

Apple-Cinnamon Smoothie, *page 57*, and Carrot-Apple-Orange Juice, *page 62*, with Veggie Pâté on yam slices, *page 76*

CHAPTER 5

Beverages

This delightful milk alternative is delicious on its own, or you can use it over cereal or porridge or in smoothies or shakes. It can also be substituted for milk in any recipe, but it does have a mild sweetness due to the dates, so you might not want to use it in savory recipes.

HOMEMADE almond milk

MAKES 4 CUPS (4 SERVINGS)

1 cup raw almonds, soaked in water for 4 hours

4 cups water

6 pitted soft dates

1. Drain and rinse the almonds. Transfer to a blender.
2. Add the water and dates.
3. Process until the almonds are very finely ground.
4. Strain into a bowl through a nut milk bag, fine-mesh strainer, or regular strainer lined with cheesecloth. Press or squeeze the solids to extract as much liquid as possible.
5. Pour into a glass jar and chill before serving. Stored in a sealed jar in the refrigerator, Homemade Almond Milk will keep for 4 days.

The Brazil nuts add selenium and other minerals to this delightful nondairy milk.

vanilla ALMOND MILK

MAKES 4 CUPS (4 SERVINGS)

1 cup raw almonds, soaked in water for 4 hours (see note)

¼ cup Brazil nuts, soaked in water for 4 hours

4 cups water

6 pitted soft dates

1 teaspoon vanilla extract

1. Drain and rinse the almonds and Brazil nuts. Transfer to a blender.
2. Add the water, dates, and vanilla extract.
3. Process until the nuts are very finely ground.
4. Strain into a bowl through a nut milk bag, fine-mesh strainer, or regular strainer lined with cheesecloth. Press or squeeze the solids to extract as much liquid as possible.
5. Pour into a glass jar and chill before serving. Stored in a sealed jar in the refrigerator, Vanilla Almond Milk will keep for 4 days.

NOTE: The almonds and Brazil nuts can be soaked together.

Sesame seeds add a significant amount of calcium to this creamy nondairy beverage.

CHOCOLATE almond milk

1 cup raw almonds, soaked in water for 4 hours

4 cups water

6 pitted soft dates

¼ cup raw white or black sesame seeds

3 tablespoons unsweetened cocoa powder

2 tablespoons maple syrup

Pinch salt

1. Drain and rinse the almonds. Transfer to a blender.
2. Add the water, dates, sesame seeds, cocoa powder, maple syrup, and salt.
3. Process until the almonds and sesame seeds are very finely ground.
4. Strain into a bowl through a nut milk bag, fine-mesh strainer, or regular strainer lined with cheesecloth. Press or squeeze the solids to extract as much liquid as possible.
5. Pour into a glass jar and chill before serving. Stored in a sealed jar in the refrigerator, Chocolate Almond Milk will keep for 4 days.

This lemonade has it all. It's tasty and looks pretty. The lemon is excellent for liver function, and the ginger improves digestion. It's also a great sports drink, thanks to the natural sugars in the dates and maple syrup and the electrolytes from the pinch of salt.

pink ginger LEMONADE

MAKES 4 CUPS (4 SERVINGS)

2 lemons

4 cups water

½ cup fresh or frozen strawberries, raspberries, or blueberries

6 pitted soft dates

2 tablespoons maple syrup

1 (1½-inch) piece fresh ginger, peeled

Pinch salt

1. Peel the lemons with a serrated knife, leaving at least some of the white pith. Cut them into chunks, removing the seeds and putting the pieces in a blender as you work.

2. Add the water, berries, dates, maple syrup, ginger, and salt to the blender and process until smooth.

3. Strain into a bowl through a medium-fine strainer.

4. Pour into a glass jar and chill before serving. Stored in a sealed jar in the refrigerator, Pink Ginger Lemonade will keep for 4 days.

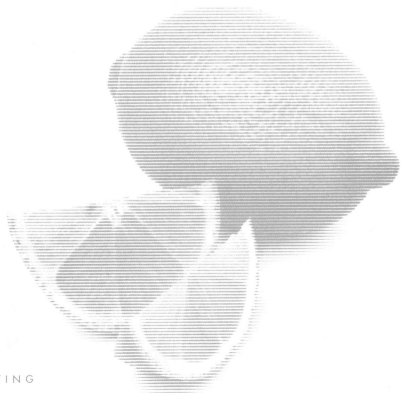

Here's a great way to enjoy a citrus juice without wasting the goodness of the fiber in the pulp and pith. Retaining some of the pith has other benefits too, as it has been shown to contain significant amounts of phytonutrients that have anti-inflammatory properties and also help lower cholesterol and blood pressure.

citrus NECTAR

3 oranges

1 grapefruit

½ cup fresh or frozen blueberries, raspberries, or strawberries

1. Peel the oranges and grapefruit with a serrated knife, leaving at least some of the white pith. Cut them into chunks, removing the seeds and putting the pieces in a blender as you work.
2. Add the berries to the blender and process until smooth.
3. Strain the mixture into a bowl through a medium-fine strainer. Serve immediately.

This refreshing hot-weather drink is a great way to use up any watermelon that might be taking up space in the refrigerator.

MELON-BERRY tango

4 cups watermelon chunks, large seeds removed

½ cup fresh or frozen blueberries, strawberries, or raspberries

½ lemon or lime with peel, coarsely chopped

1. Combine all the ingredients in a blender and process until smooth.
2. Strain into a bowl through a medium-fine strainer. Pour into glasses and serve immediately.

Variation: Replace the watermelon with other types of melon, such as cantaloupe or honeydew.

Even though green smoothies are a beneficial addition to a whole-foods diet, it's fun to have fruit-only smoothies sometimes. This is a great starter smoothie for children or even grown-ups new to the world of whole foods, who might be a little suspicious of green smoothies.

CREAMY fruit shake

MAKES 2 SERVINGS

2 frozen bananas (see note) or fresh bananas, broken into pieces

1 cup freshly squeezed orange juice (about 2 oranges)

1 cup Homemade Almond Milk (page 52) or other nondairy milk, plus more as needed

1 cup fresh or frozen strawberries or raspberries

6 pitted soft dates

6 ice cubes

Combine all the ingredients in a blender and process until smooth. Add more almond milk as necessary to thin to the desired consistency. Serve immediately.

NOTE: Frozen bananas are great to keep on hand for blending up a quick shake anytime. Before you freeze them, be sure they're ripe. Then simply peel them and store them in a ziplock bag or other container in the freezer.

This deeply satisfying meal in a glass is perfect for an active lifestyle. The tahini and dates make it rich in calcium and iron.

turbo SHAKE

MAKES 1 LARGE OR 2 SMALL SERVINGS

2 frozen bananas (see note above) or fresh bananas, broken into pieces

1 cup water, plus more as needed

6 pitted soft dates

2 tablespoons maple syrup

1½ tablespoons unsweetened cocoa or carob powder

1 heaping tablespoon tahini

Pinch salt

Combine all the ingredients in a blender and process until smooth. Add more water if necessary to thin to the desired consistency. Serve immediately.

If you live in a northern climate, local fruit can be hard to find when summer has come and gone. Here's an apple-based smoothie made with warming cinnamon that is superb through the fall and winter. Barley grass powder or wheatgrass powder is an optional ingredient, but highly recommended for its concentrated nutrients. Look for both in the supplements aisle at natural food stores.

APPLE-CINNAMON smoothie

See photo facing page 51.

MAKES 1 LARGE OR 2 SMALL SERVINGS

2 apples with peel, coarsely chopped

2 cups baby spinach, lightly packed

1 cup water, plus more as needed

½ cup unsweetened apple juice

1 large stalk celery, coarsely chopped

4 pitted soft dates

1 tablespoon ground chia seeds or flaxseeds

1 teaspoon barley grass powder or wheatgrass powder (optional)

¾ teaspoon ground cinnamon

Combine all the ingredients in a blender and process until smooth. Add more water if necessary to thin to the desired consistency. Serve immediately.

This blended drink is perfect for mornings when you want a light but wholesome and warming breakfast. The spirulina powder is optional, but this superfood will provide a big boost in nutrients, so give it a try. You can find it in the supplements section at natural food stores.

pear-ginger SMOOTHIE

MAKES 1 LARGE OR 2 SMALL SERVINGS

2 pears with peel, coarsely chopped

2 cups baby spinach, lightly packed

1 cup water, plus more as needed

½ cup unsweetened apple juice

1 leaf Swiss chard, coarsely chopped (optional)

3 pitted soft dates

1 tablespoon freshly squeezed lemon juice

1 tablespoon ground flaxseeds

1 (1-inch) piece fresh ginger, peeled

1 teaspoon spirulina powder (optional)

Combine all the ingredients in a blender and process until smooth. Add more water if necessary to thin to the desired consistency. Serve immediately.

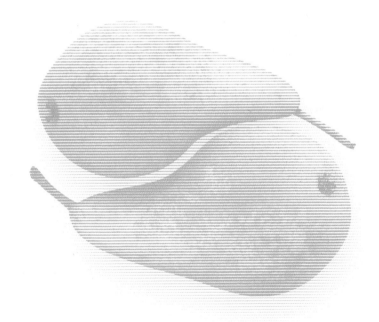

Green smoothies are fruit-based blender drinks with added greens. They can be consumed as a meal and are perfect for getting more greens and minerals into your diet in a delicious and highly digestible way. You can make one in the morning and take it with you to work or school in a thermos or glass jar for an instant meal. Barley grass powder or wheatgrass powder is an optional ingredient, but highly recommended for its concentrated nutrients. Look for both in the supplements aisle at natural food stores.

fruity green SMOOTHIE

MAKES 1 LARGE OR 2 SMALL SERVINGS

2 cups baby spinach, lightly packed

2 frozen bananas (see note, page 56) or fresh bananas, broken into pieces

1 cup fresh or frozen strawberries, blueberries, or raspberries

1 apple with peel, coarsely chopped

Juice of 2 oranges, or 1 cup unsweetened apple juice

½ cup water, plus more as needed

4 pitted soft dates

1 tablespoon barley grass powder or wheatgrass powder (optional)

Combine all the ingredients in a blender and process until smooth. Add more water if necessary to thin to the desired consistency. Serve immediately.

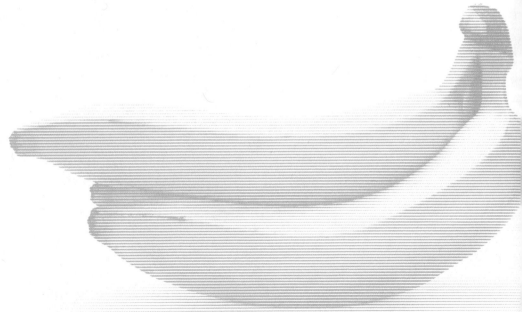

Many health-conscious people are falling in love with edible wild plants. They're loaded with nutrition and have superior detoxifying properties, and they're usually free. To learn more about them, I suggest the book *Edible Wild Plants*, by John Kallas. Once you feel confident that you can identify various edible plants, look for them in your yard or garden or when you're out walking in natural environments (so you can be sure they haven't been exposed to herbicides or other noxious chemicals).

WILD GREENS smoothie

MAKES 1 LARGE OR 2 SMALL SERVINGS

3 peaches with peel, coarsely chopped

2 cups wild greens (such as dandelion, mallow, purslane, stinging nettle leaves, or wild spinach), **lightly packed**

Juice of 2 oranges

1 cup fresh or frozen blueberries

1 cup water, plus more as needed

4 pitted soft dates

Combine all the ingredients in a blender and process until smooth. Add more water if necessary to thin to the desired consistency. Serve immediately.

This is a quick alternative to a fresh salad. Just blend and eat—or, rather, drink!

BLENDED salad

3 cups baby spinach, lightly packed

½ cucumber, peeled and coarsely chopped

1 tomato, coarsely chopped

1 small apple with peel, coarsely chopped

1 celery stalk, coarsely chopped

½ red bell pepper, coarsely chopped

½ cup water

¼ teaspoon salt

Combine all the ingredients in a blender and process until smooth. Add more water if necessary to thin to the desired consistency. Serve immediately.

NOTE: Buy red bell peppers in summer, when they're in season and affordable. Cut them in half, remove the seeds and membranes, and freeze them in ziplock bags. They can be used in blended salads and any recipe in which they will be cooked.

Italian Blended Salad: Add 6 basil leaves and 1 small clove of garlic.

Mexican Blended Salad: Add ¼ cup of cilantro and ½ avocado.

This juice is truly heavenly. Sweet juices like this one should ideally be consumed about twenty minutes prior to or after physical activity so their abundant natural sugars can be readily used by the body.

carrot-apple-orange JUICE

See photo facing page 51.

3 oranges, peeled with a knife

8 carrots, scrubbed

2 apples with peel, cored

1. Peel the oranges with a serrated knife, leaving at least some of the white pith. Cut them into chunks and remove the seeds.
2. Cut the carrots and apples into sizes appropriate for your juicer.
3. Run the prepared fruits and carrots through the juicer, alternating the softer oranges and apple with the denser carrots and finishing with carrot; this will help keep the juicer's blades and screens clean. Serve immediately.

This sweet, rich, and vibrantly orange juice is enhanced with a hint of fennel. It also makes great use of fennel stems and leaves, which are rarely used in recipes calling for the fennel bulb.

FENNEL ambrosia

2 oranges

4 carrots, scrubbed

2 apples with peel, cored

3 fennel stems with leaves

1. Peel the oranges with a serrated knife, leaving at least some of the white pith. Cut them into chunks and remove the seeds.
2. Cut the carrots, apples, and fennel stems into sizes appropriate for your juicer.
3. Run the prepared fruits and vegetables through the juicer, alternating the softer oranges and apples with the denser carrots and fennel stems and finishing with carrot; this will help keep the juicer's blades and screens clean. Serve immediately.

Green juices are freshly pressed through a juicer and made primarily from green vegetables, particularly celery, cucumber, and leafy greens such as romaine lettuce, kale, Swiss chard, spinach, dandelion greens, or collard greens. The lemon and apple in this recipe brighten the flavor and help take the edge off the bitterness of the greens, making it ideal for people new to green juices.

fresh GREEN JUICE

MAKES 2 SERVINGS

1 small lemon

4 stalks celery

1 apple with peel, cored

½ cucumber, peeled

4 leaves romaine lettuce, kale, Swiss chard, dandelion greens, or collard greens, or a combination

1. Peel the lemon with a serrated knife, leaving at least some of the white pith. Cut it into chunks and remove the seeds.

2. Cut the celery, apple, cucumber, and lettuce into sizes appropriate sizes for your juicer.

3. Run the prepared fruits and vegetables through the juicer, alternating the softer items (lemon, apple, and cucumber) with the denser celery and leafy greens and finishing with celery; this will help keep the juicer's blades and screens clean. Serve immediately.

This is the perfect juice to make in the summertime when tomatoes and other vegetables are abundant and fresh.

eight-vegetable JUICE

MAKES 2 SERVINGS

3 carrots, scrubbed

2 large tomatoes

3 stalks celery

1 small beet, scrubbed

½ cup coarsely chopped cabbage

½ red bell pepper

1 green onion, trimmed

2 cups baby spinach, lightly packed

Salt (optional)

1. Cut the carrots, tomatoes, celery, beet, cabbage, bell pepper, and green onion into sizes appropriate for your juicer.

2. Run the prepared vegetables and spinach through the juicer, alternating the softer vegetables (tomatoes, spinach, bell pepper, and green onion) with the denser vegetables (carrots, celery, beet, and cabbage) and finishing with carrot; this will help keep the juicer's blades and screens clean. Stir in salt to taste if desired. Serve immediately.

Dips and Spreads

This is a fresh, zesty dip for corn chips and the perfect condiment to complement any number of Mexican or Southwestern dishes.

tomato-corn SALSA

MAKES 3 CUPS

2 cups diced tomatoes

½ cup cooked fresh corn kernels or thawed frozen corn

⅓ cup finely chopped red or Vidalia onion

3 inches cucumber, peeled, seeded, and finely diced

¼ cup finely chopped fresh cilantro

2 teaspoons minced garlic

1 teaspoon cider vinegar

1 teaspoon extra-virgin olive oil

1 teaspoon maple syrup

¼ teaspoon salt

⅛ teaspoon ground cumin

1. Combine all the ingredients in a medium bowl. Let sit at room temperature for 1 to 4 hours for the flavors to meld. Serve chilled or at room temperature.

2. Stored in a sealed container in the refrigerator, Tomato-Corn Salsa will keep for 4 days.

Chunky Guacamole is a versatile way to prepare avocados, which are rich in healthful fats. Serve it with baked corn chips or as a topping for Taco Salad with Chili (page 143). Or try a simple raw burrito: spoon the Chunky Guacamole into romaine lettuce leaves and enjoy! Although the dulse is optional, it's highly recommended for its excellent nutritional profile. Like all sea vegetables, it's high in trace minerals. Look for dulse at natural food stores.

CHUNKY guacamole

MAKES 2 CUPS

3 ripe avocados, cubed (see note) **or flesh scooped out**

¼ cup freshly squeezed lemon juice (about 1 large lemon)

2 cloves garlic, minced

1 tablespoon dulse flakes (optional)

1 teaspoon salt

1 small tomato, diced

½ small yellow bell pepper, diced

2 tablespoons finely chopped green onion

1. Put the avocados in a medium bowl and mash with a fork or potato masher until uniformly chunky.

2. Add the lemon juice, garlic, optional dulse, and salt and continue mashing until creamy but some texture still remains.

3. Stir in the tomato, bell pepper, and green onion. Serve immediately.

NOTE: To cube an avocado, cut the avocado in half lengthwise and remove the pit by striking it firmly with the sharp edge of a chef's knife. The knife blade should embed in the pit, which can now be removed with a twist of the knife. Then use the tip of the knife to score the avocado flesh in both directions. Scoop the flesh out with a spoon.

This creamy green party dip is delightful served with whole-grain crackers.

CREAMY spinach-basil spread

1 cup raw cashews, soaked in water for 4 hours (see note)

2 cups baby spinach, lightly packed

¼ cup fresh basil leaves, lightly packed and coarsely chopped

1 small clove garlic, minced

3 tablespoons extra-virgin olive oil

2 tablespoons water

1½ tablespoons freshly squeezed lemon juice

1 tablespoon nutritional yeast (optional)

1 teaspoon cider vinegar

½ teaspoon salt

1. Drain and rinse the cashews. Transfer to a food processor and process until finely ground.

2. Add the spinach, basil, and garlic and pulse several times, until finely chopped.

3. Add the oil, water, lemon juice, optional nutritional yeast, vinegar, and salt and process until well combined, stopping occasionally to scrape down the work bowl with a rubber spatula and move the mixture to the blades. Don't overprocess; the spread should retain some texture.

4. Transfer to a small serving bowl, cover, and refrigerate until ready to serve. Serve chilled or at room temperature.

5. Stored in a sealed container in the refrigerator, Creamy Spinach-Basil Spread will keep for 4 days.

NOTE: Soaking the cashews is optional but will result in a creamier spread. If you don't have time to soak them or are using a high-powered blender, you can skip this step.

This pungent and flavorful spread is excellent served on whole-grain toast alongside a hearty bowl of soup. You'll undoubtedly find numerous other ways to use it, including in Cheesy Vegetable Pie (page 136).

lemony tomato TAPENADE

MAKES 1½ CUPS

1 cup sun-dried tomatoes, soaked in water for 1 hour

2 cloves garlic, minced

1½ tablespoons freshly squeezed lemon juice

1½ teaspoons grated lemon zest

1½ teaspoons chopped fresh thyme, or ¾ teaspoon dried

½ cup extra-virgin olive oil

1 teaspoon maple syrup

Salt (optional)

1. Drain the sun-dried tomatoes. Transfer to a food processor and process until finely chopped.

2. Add the garlic, lemon juice, lemon zest, and thyme and process until finely chopped, stopping occasionally to scrape down the work bowl with a rubber spatula and move the mixture to the blades. Don't overprocess; the mixture should retain some texture.

3. Add the oil and maple syrup and pulse several times to combine.

4. Season with salt to taste if desired. Sun-dried tomatoes are often preserved with salt, so this will affect the amount of salt needed. Transfer the mixture to a small serving bowl. Serve chilled or at room temperature.

5. Stored in a sealed container in the refrigerator, Lemony Tomato Tapenade will keep for 2 weeks.

Hummus is a great staple food in a plant-based diet. It's easy to make, deeply satisfying, and packed with protein. For a quick, health-supporting meal, let your family or guests fill whole-grain wraps with generous portions of Heavenly Hummus and their choice of tomatoes, cucumbers, lettuce, sprouts, and other vegetables. For a special treat, you might also offer grilled zucchini and red bell peppers.

HEAVENLY hummus

MAKES 2 CUPS

1½ cups cooked or canned chickpeas, liquid reserved

¼ cup freshly squeezed lemon juice (about 1 large lemon)

1 clove garlic, coarsely chopped

¼ cup tahini

¼ teaspoon salt

¼ teaspoon ground cumin

¼ cup chopped fresh parsley, for garnish

Extra-virgin olive oil, for drizzling (optional)

1. Put the chickpeas, lemon juice, and garlic in a blender or food processor and process until almost smooth. Add the tahini, salt, cumin, and ¼ cup of reserved bean liquid or water and process until smooth. Add more bean liquid or water if necessary to thin to the desired consistency.

2. Transfer to a small serving bowl. Serve chilled or at room temperature. Just before serving, garnish with the chopped parsley and a drizzle of olive oil if desired.

3. Stored in a sealed container in the refrigerator, Heavenly Hummus will keep for 5 days.

Serve this lively dip with baked corn chips or whole-grain pita wedges for an easy-to-prepare snack that hits the spot. For a layered dip, try topping it with Tomato-Corn Salsa (page 66).

creamy white BEAN DIP

¼ cup coarsely chopped red onion

¼ cup chopped fresh parsley or cilantro, plus more for garnish

1 teaspoon minced garlic

1½ cups cooked or canned cannellini beans, rinsed if canned

2 tablespoons extra-virgin olive oil, plus more for drizzling

1 tablespoon cider vinegar

1 tablespoon freshly squeezed lemon juice

½ teaspoon chili powder

½ teaspoon salt

¼ teaspoon ground cumin

Dash hot sauce (optional)

1. Put the onion, parsley, and garlic in a food processor and process until finely chopped.

2. Add the beans, oil, vinegar, lemon juice, chili powder, salt, cumin, and optional hot sauce and process until mostly smooth, stopping occasionally to scrape down the work bowl with a rubber spatula and move the mixture to the blades. Don't overprocess; the dip should retain some texture.

3. Transfer to a small serving bowl. Serve chilled or at room temperature. Just before serving, garnish with chopped parsley and a drizzle of olive oil if desired.

4. Stored in a sealed container in the refrigerator, Creamy White Bean Dip will keep for 5 days.

Tofu Cottage Cheese can be spread on crackers, stuffed into celery stalks, or dolloped over a fresh salad for a protein-rich addition to any meal.

TOFU cottage cheese

MAKES 2 CUPS

1 pound firm tofu

2 tablespoons extra-virgin olive oil

2 tablespoons freshly squeezed lemon juice

2 tablespoons nutritional yeast

1 tablespoon cider vinegar

¾ teaspoon salt

1 green onion, halved lengthwise and thinly sliced, or 3 tablespoons finely chopped fresh chives

1 teaspoon dried dill weed

1. Put half of the tofu in a blender or food processor. Add the oil, lemon juice, nutritional yeast, vinegar, and salt and process until thick and creamy.

2. Put the remaining tofu in a medium bowl and mash with a fork or potato masher. Add the blended tofu mixture, onion, and dill weed and stir to combine. Serve chilled or at room temperature.

3. Stored in a sealed container in the refrigerator, Tofu Cottage Cheese will keep for 5 days.

A somewhat unusual combination of seasonings give this spread a pleasing allure. Try it on rice cakes or whole-grain toast.

tofu SALAD SPREAD

1 pound firm tofu

½ cup vegan mayonnaise

1 tablespoon nutritional yeast

1 teaspoon ground turmeric

1 teaspoon curry powder

¾ teaspoon ground coriander

½ teaspoon salt

⅓ cup finely chopped celery

2 green onions, halved lengthwise and thinly sliced

1. Crumble the tofu into a medium bowl. Add the vegan mayonnaise, nutritional yeast, turmeric, curry powder, coriander, and salt. Mash with a fork or a potato masher until evenly combined.

2. Stir in the celery and green onions. Serve chilled or at room temperature.

3. Stored in a sealed container in the refrigerator, Tofu Salad Spread will keep for 5 days.

This smooth and savory pâté makes a delightful party appetizer when served on whole-grain crackers. If you can find them, use cremini mushrooms, which are closely related to common button mushrooms but have darker flesh and a deeper, richer flavor.

ALMOND-MUSHROOM pâté

MAKES 2 CUPS

1 cup raw almonds, blanched (see notes)

4 tablespoons extra-virgin olive oil

6 cups halved and sliced cremini or button mushrooms

¼ cup finely chopped leek (see notes) **or sweet onion**

1 teaspoon chopped fresh thyme, or ½ teaspoon dried

1 teaspoon maple syrup

1 teaspoon cider vinegar

¾ teaspoon salt

¼ teaspoon ground pepper

Chopped fresh parsley, for garnish

1. Put the almonds in a food processor and process until finely ground. Leave them in the food processor.

2. Put 2 tablespoons of the oil and the mushrooms and leek in a large skillet. Cook and stir over medium heat until the mushrooms are slightly browned and the liquid evaporates, about 15 minutes.

3. Add the thyme, maple syrup, vinegar, salt, and pepper and cook over medium-low heat, stirring occasionally, until the mushrooms are almost completely dry, about 15 minutes.

4. Add the mushroom mixture and remaining 2 tablespoons of oil to the almonds in the food processor. Process until smooth, stopping occasionally to scrape down the work bowl with a rubber spatula and move the mixture to the blades.

5. Transfer to a serving bowl, cover, and chill for at least 1 hour. Garnish with parsley just before serving.

6. Stored in a sealed container in the refrigerator, Almond-Mushroom Pâté will keep for 5 days.

NOTES

- To blanch the almonds, put them in a medium heatproof bowl. Add about 2 cups of boiling water. Let sit for 1 minute, then drain and rinse with cold water. Rub the almonds between your thumb and fingers to slip off the skins. Discard the skins.
- Take care when cleaning leeks, as they tend to have a lot of sand between the leaves. First, cut off the topmost dark green portion of the leeks. Then slice the leeks in half lengthwise from the top toward the root end, leaving about ½ inch uncut at the root end so that the leaves stay together. Run them under water, separating the leaves to remove all traces of dirt. Start slicing from the root end, removing medium to dark green leaves as you go along and using only the white and pale green parts. The dark green leaves can be used in Vegetable Broth (page 78).

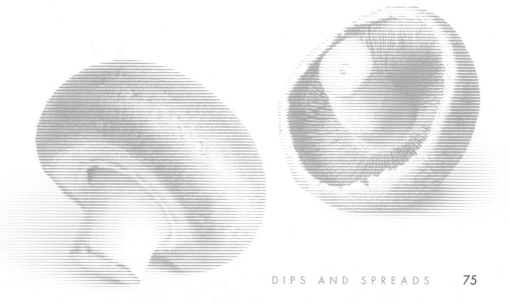

Try this wonderful raw pâté on raw sweet potato crackers. Just peel a sweet potato and slice it into paper-thin circles shortly before serving. (A mandoline works well for this.) Shape the pâté into a mound on a serving plate with the sweet potato slices surrounding it and garnish with parsley sprigs.

VEGGIE pâté

See photo facing page 19.

MAKES 1½ CUPS

1 cup raw sunflower seeds, soaked in water for 4 hours

1 carrot, scrubbed and coarsely chopped

½ cup coarsely chopped fresh parsley

1 clove garlic, minced

2 tablespoons freshly squeezed lemon juice

1½ tablespoons light miso

1 stalk celery, finely chopped

Salt

1. Drain and rinse the sunflower seeds. Transfer to a food processor.

2. Add the carrot, parsley, and garlic and process until finely chopped, stopping occasionally to scrape down the work bowl with a rubber spatula and move the mixture to the blades. Don't overprocess; the mixture should still retain some texture.

3. Add the lemon juice and miso and process until well combined.

4. Transfer to a bowl and stir in the celery. Season with salt to taste. Serve chilled or at room temperature.

5. Stored in a sealed container in the refrigerator, Veggie Pâté will keep for 2 days.

NOTE: There is often confusion around the difference between a sweet potato and a yam. In North America, many supermarkets call what is actually a sweet potato a yam, so this adds to the confusion. Yams are actually rarely found in supermarkets. They have dark beige skin and pale yellow flesh. Sweet potatoes have reddish skin and deep orange flesh.

CHAPTER 7

Soups

Homemade vegetable broth is a great way to use up not-so-fresh vegetables. Enjoy it on its own sipped from a mug, or use it as a rich base for soups or as the cooking liquid for grains.

VEGETABLE broth

8 cups water, plus more as needed

2 onions, coarsely chopped

2 potatoes, scrubbed and coarsely chopped

2 carrots, scrubbed and coarsely chopped

2 stalks celery with leaves, coarsely chopped

2 leeks (see note, page 75)**, chopped** (optional)

½ cup chopped fresh parsley

2 bay leaves

1. Put the water, onions, potatoes, carrots, celery, optional leeks, parsley, and bay leaves in a large soup pot over high heat. Add more water if necessary to cover the vegetables by 3 inches. Bring to a boil. Decrease the heat to medium-low, cover, and simmer for 3 hours.

2. Strain through a colander set over a large bowl. Pour the broth through a fine-mesh strainer to remove any remaining solids.

3. Stored in a sealed container, Vegetable Broth will keep for 3 days in the refrigerator or 3 months in the freezer. If freezing the broth, you may want to store it in smaller containers so you can thaw just the amount needed for recipes.

NOTE: Feel free to use any additional vegetables that you have on hand in this broth. However, if you're using the broth as a base for soups, it's best to avoid strong-tasting vegetables like broccoli, cabbage, cauliflower, or garlic.

Miso soup is a light and delicate starter for Asian-style meals. To benefit from the health-promoting friendly bacteria that miso contains, look for unpasteurized varieties and be sure not to boil the soup once the miso has been added.

asian MISO SOUP

5 cups water

¼ cup arame

⅔ cup thinly sliced cabbage

⅓ cup scrubbed and finely diced carrot

⅓ cup finely diced celery

¼ cup dark miso

4 tablespoons thinly sliced green onions or chopped fresh chives, for garnish

4 teaspoons gomasio (preferably homemade, page 122) **or sesame seeds, for garnish**

4 teaspoons tahini (optional)

1. Put the water and arame in a soup pot and bring to a boil over high heat. Decrease the heat to medium-low, cover, and simmer for 5 minutes.

2. Add the cabbage, carrot, and celery, cover, and simmer until the vegetables are tender-crisp, about 3 minutes. Remove from the heat.

3. Transfer ⅔ cup of the liquid to a cup. Add the miso and stir to form a smooth paste. Stir the miso mixture into the soup.

4. Serve immediately, garnishing each serving with 1 tablespoon of the green onions and 1 teaspoon of the gomasio. Offer the optional tahini at the table for stirring into individual servings of soup if desired.

5. Stored in a sealed container in the refrigerator, Asian Miso Soup will keep for 3 days. Warm it gently over low heat before serving.

Variation: Any vegetables you have on hand can be added to this soup. Good options include broccoli florets or thinly sliced kohlrabi, daikon radish, or burdock root.

This is a great recipe to use when trying out unfamiliar greens because even those that are bitter or tough when raw tend to become sweet and tender in this recipe. Try using a combination of greens or mixing in some nutrient-rich wild greens, such as garlic mustard, stinging nettle, or wild spinach. This soup is loaded with calcium and iron, thanks to the tahini and the greens, which are one of nature's best sources of minerals. For a hearty meal, spoon this soup over steamed and quartered new potatoes.

GARLICKY greens soup

MAKES 4 SERVINGS

4 cups water or vegetable broth (preferably homemade, page 78)

1 leek, halved lengthwise and sliced (see note, page 75)

6 cloves garlic, peeled and minced, or ½ cup finely chopped garlic scapes (see note)

5 to 6 cups stemmed and chopped leafy greens (such as kale, rapini, spinach, Swiss chard, or wild greens), **lightly packed**

3 tablespoons light or dark miso

Salt (optional)

4 tablespoons tahini

4 tablespoons chopped green onion or fresh chives

1. Put the water, leek, and garlic in a soup pot and bring to a boil over high heat. Decrease the heat to medium-low, cover, and simmer for 8 minutes.

2. Add the greens. Cover and simmer, stirring occasionally, until the greens are tender, between 5 and 20 minutes depending on the type of greens used. Remove from the heat.

3. Transfer about ½ cup of the liquid to a cup. Add the miso and stir to form a smooth paste. Stir the miso mixture into the soup.

4. Season with salt to taste if desired. Serve hot, spooning 1 tablespoon of the tahini into each serving and garnishing each with 1 tablespoon of the green onion.

5. Stored in a sealed container in the refrigerator, Garlicky Greens Soup will keep for 3 days.

NOTE: Garlic scapes are the curly tops of young garlic plants. They're available at most farmers' markets in spring and early summer.

This delicately flavored soup is surprisingly creamy. It's a great way to use up summer's abundance of zucchini.

creamy zucchini SOUP

2 tablespoons extra-virgin olive oil

Water or vegetable broth (preferably homemade, page 78)

1½ cups sliced leeks (see note, page 75) **or chopped onions**

8 cups coarsely chopped green or yellow zucchini or a combination

½ cup coarsely chopped fresh parsley

Salt

Ground pepper

1. Put the oil, ½ cup of the water, and the leeks in a soup pot over medium heat. Cook, stirring frequently, for 10 minutes.

2. Add the zucchini, parsley, and just enough water to reach about 1 inch below the vegetables. (Zucchini releases a lot of moisture as it cooks, so don't add too much water or the finished soup will be too thin.) Decrease the heat to medium-low, cover, and simmer, stirring occasionally, until the zucchini is very tender, 12 to 15 minutes.

3. Using a conventional blender and working in batches or using a hand blender, process the mixture until very smooth.

4. Season with salt and pepper to taste. Serve hot.

5. Stored in a sealed container, Creamy Zucchini Soup will keep for 3 days in the refrigerator or 3 months in the freezer.

Creamy Zucchini-Spinach Soup: Add about 4 cups of coarsely chopped spinach, lightly packed, when adding the zucchini.

The secret to this crowd-pleasing soup is blending part of the cooked soup with raw cashews to create a sweet creaminess.

CASHEW corn chowder

See photo on facing page.

6 cups water or vegetable broth (preferably homemade, page 78)

3 cups scrubbed and diced potatoes (about 3 medium potatoes)

1½ cups chopped onions or sliced leeks (see note, page 75)

2 stalks celery with leaves, halved lengthwise and sliced

4 cups fresh or frozen corn kernels

1 cup finely chopped fresh parsley

1 teaspoon dried dill weed

1 teaspoon salt

½ teaspoon dried tarragon

½ cup raw cashews

Ground pepper (optional)

1. Put the water, potatoes, onions, and celery in a soup pot and bring to a boil over high heat. Decrease the heat to medium-low, cover, and simmer, stirring occasionally, until the vegetables are almost tender, about 15 minutes.

2. Stir in the corn, parsley, dill weed, salt, and tarragon and simmer, stirring occasionally, until all the vegetables are tender, about 10 minutes. Let cool slightly.

3. Put the cashews in a blender. Add 3 cups of the cooled potato mixture and process until completely smooth.

4. Pour the cashew mixture into the soup pot. Cook over medium heat, stirring occasionally, until steaming hot.

5. Season with pepper to taste if desired. Serve hot.

6. Stored in a sealed container in the refrigerator, Cashew Corn Chowder will keep for 3 days.

Cashew Corn Chowder, *facing page*

Cabbage Salad with Apple, Pecans, and Raisins, *page 101*

This is a lovely blended fall and winter soup with an intriguing combination of sweet and spicy flavors.

curried winter squash SOUP

4 cups peeled and coarsely chopped butternut squash (about 1 medium squash) **or other winter squash**

2 apples, peeled and chopped

1½ cups chopped leeks (see note, page 75) **or onions**

2 cloves garlic, minced

1 (1-inch) piece fresh ginger, peeled and grated

3 cups water or vegetable broth (preferably homemade, page 78), **plus more as needed**

2 tablespoons cold-pressed coconut oil

1½ tablespoons reduced-sodium tamari

1 tablespoon maple syrup

2 teaspoons ground coriander

1 teaspoon ground cumin

1 teaspoon ground turmeric

¾ teaspoon ground cinnamon

Salt (optional)

1. Put the squash, apples, leeks, garlic, and ginger in a soup pot. Add the water. It should just cover the vegetables; if it doesn't, add more water as needed. Bring to a boil over high heat. Decrease the heat to medium-low, cover, and simmer, stirring occasionally, until the squash is fork-tender, about 15 minutes.

2. Stir in the oil, tamari, maple syrup, coriander, cumin, turmeric, and cinnamon. Simmer, stirring occasionally, for 10 minutes.

3. Using a conventional blender and working in batches or using a hand blender, process the mixture until smooth.

4. Season with salt to taste if desired. Serve hot.

5. Stored in a sealed container, Curried Winter Squash Soup will keep for 3 days in the refrigerator or 3 months in the freezer.

One of the best ways to get people excited about legumes, which are an essential part of a balanced vegetarian diet, is through delicious, hearty soups, and this one is a winner every time. Legumes sometimes have a dry texture; using them in soups makes them creamy and moist and also allows them to absorb the flavors of the broth. In exchange, they add richness to the broth and make for a filling soup.

sweet-and-sour LENTIL SOUP

MAKES 4 TO 6 SERVINGS

1 cup brown, green, or French lentils, soaked in water for 8 hours

6 cups water or vegetable broth (preferably homemade, page 78), **plus more as needed**

1½ cups finely chopped leeks (see note, page 75) **or onions**

1 carrot, scrubbed and finely chopped

1 stalk celery, finely chopped

4 cloves garlic, minced

1 can (14 ounces) tomato purée or tomato sauce

1 teaspoon chopped fresh thyme, or ½ teaspoon dried

1½ tablespoons balsamic vinegar

1½ tablespoons maple syrup

1 teaspoon salt

1. Drain and rinse the lentils. Transfer to a soup pot and add the water, leeks, carrot, celery, and garlic. Bring to a boil over high heat. Decrease the heat to medium-low, cover, and simmer, stirring occasionally, until the lentils are tender, about 40 minutes.

2. Stir in the tomato purée and thyme and simmer for 10 minutes, adding more water if needed to maintain a soupy consistency.

3. Stir in the vinegar, maple syrup, and salt. Serve hot.

4. Stored in a sealed container, Sweet-and-Sour Lentil Soup will keep for 3 days in the refrigerator or 3 months in the freezer.

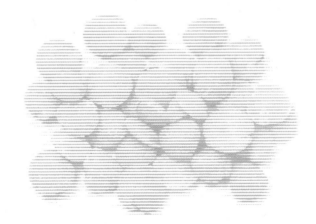

This is vegetarian version of a French Canadian classic. The sweet potato gives it a satisfying sweetness.

GOLDEN SPLIT PEA soup

MAKES 6 SERVINGS

1½ cups yellow split peas, soaked in water for 8 hours

6 cups water

1½ cups diced onion

1 large sweet potato, peeled and chopped (about 1½ cups)

2 carrots, scrubbed and diced

2 stalks celery with leaves, diced

1 teaspoon dried oregano

2 bay leaves

1 teaspoon salt

1. Drain and rinse the split peas. Transfer to a soup pot and add the water, onion, sweet potato, carrots, celery, oregano, and bay leaves. Bring to a boil over high heat. Decrease the heat to medium-low, cover, and simmer, stirring occasionally, until the split peas are tender and falling apart, about 1½ hours.

2. Stir in the salt. Using a conventional blender and working in batches or using a hand blender, process the mixture until smooth. Alternatively, for a soup with some texture, simply mash the mixture in the pot with a potato masher to achieve the desired consistency. Serve hot.

3. Stored in a sealed container, Golden Split Pea Soup will keep for 3 days in the refrigerator or 3 months in the freezer.

This is a one-bowl meal that warms the soul.

KALE AND navy bean soup

MAKES 4 TO 6 SERVINGS

2 tablespoons extra-virgin olive oil

6 cups water or vegetable broth
(preferably homemade, page 78)

1½ cups diced onions or sliced leeks
(see note, page 75)

1 large carrot, scrubbed, halved
lengthwise, and sliced

1 large stalk celery with leaves,
halved lengthwise and sliced

6 cups stemmed and coarsely
chopped green or red kale, lightly
packed

1½ cups cooked or canned navy
beans

2 tablespoons reduced-sodium tamari

4 teaspoons chopped fresh thyme, or
2 teaspoons dried

½ teaspoon salt

Nut Parmesan (page 122; optional)

1. Put the oil, ½ cup of the water, and the onions, carrot, and celery in a soup pot over medium heat. Cook, stirring frequently, until the vegetables begin to soften, about 5 minutes.

2. Add the kale and cook, stirring frequently, for 5 minutes.

3. Add the remaining 5½ cups of water and the beans, tamari, and thyme and bring to a boil over high heat. Decrease the heat to medium-low, cover, and simmer, stirring occasionally, until the kale is tender, about 15 minutes.

4. Stir in the salt. Serve hot, sprinkling each serving with Nut Parmesan if desired.

5. Stored in a sealed container, Kale and Navy Bean Soup will keep for 3 days in the refrigerator or 3 months in the freezer.

This hearty soup has an exotic flavor and is even better the next day. Black beans have the highest anti-oxidant level of any beans as indicated by their dark color, which hints at high amounts of flavonoids, a group of antioxidants known to slow the aging process and reduce the risk of degenerative diseases.

black bean SOUP

2 tablespoons extra-virgin olive oil

½ cup water

1 large onion, finely chopped

2 carrots, scrubbed and grated

2 stalks celery, finely chopped

¼ cup chopped fresh parsley

2 cloves garlic, minced

8 cups bean cooking liquid, vegetable broth (preferably homemade, page 78), water, or a combination

5 cups cooked or canned black beans, liquid reserved

3 tablespoons blackstrap molasses

3 tablespoons reduced-sodium tamari

2 teaspoons ground cumin

2 teaspoons ground coriander

1½ teaspoons salt

½ teaspoon ground cloves

¼ teaspoon cayenne or hot sauce (optional)

Chopped fresh parsley or cilantro, for garnish

Chopped green onions or fresh chives, for garnish

1. Put the oil, water, onion, carrots, celery, parsley, and garlic in a soup pot over medium heat. Cook, stirring frequently, until the vegetables are tender, about 8 minutes.

2. Stir in the bean cooking liquid, beans, molasses, tamari, cumin, coriander, salt, cloves, and optional cayenne and bring to a boil. Decrease the heat to medium-low, cover, and cook, stirring occasionally, for 30 minutes.

3. Serve hot, garnished with parsley and green onions.

4. Stored in a sealed container, Black Bean Soup will keep for 3 days in the refrigerator or 3 months in the freezer.

This flavorful chili is a welcome warming meal on a cold evening. It's substantial enough to serve as a main dish, perhaps with a crisp green salad on the side. Or try it in Taco Salad with Chili (page 143).

zesty bean CHILI

MAKES 10 CUPS (6 TO 8 SERVINGS)

2 tablespoons extra-virgin olive oil

¼ cup water, plus more as needed

2 onions, finely chopped

1 carrot, scrubbed and finely chopped

1 red bell pepper, diced

1 stalk celery with leaves, finely chopped

2 tablespoons minced garlic

2 tablespoons chili powder

2 teaspoons ground cumin

2 teaspoons dried oregano

⅛ teaspoon cayenne, or dash hot sauce, plus more as desired

4½ cups cooked or canned red kidney beans, liquid reserved

1 large can (28 ounces) crushed tomatoes

1 can (6 ounces) tomato paste

2 bay leaves

Bean cooking liquid, vegetable broth (preferably homemade, page 78), or water, as needed

1½ cups frozen or fresh corn kernels (optional)

2 tablespoons unrefined cane sugar

2 tablespoons reduced-sodium tamari

2 tablespoons cider vinegar

1½ teaspoons salt

1. Put the oil, water, onions, carrot, bell pepper, celery, and garlic in a soup pot over medium heat. Cook, stirring frequently, until all the vegetables are tender, 7 to 10 minutes, adding more water if necessary to prevent sticking.

2. Stir in the chili powder, cumin, oregano, and cayenne and cook, stirring frequently, for 5 minutes.

3. Stir in the beans, tomatoes, tomato paste, and bay leaves. Add enough bean cooking liquid to cover by 1 inch. Decrease the heat to medium-low and simmer uncovered, stirring occasionally, for 1½ hours.

4. Stir in the optional corn and the sugar, tamari, vinegar, and salt and simmer for 10 minutes.

5. Remove the bay leaves. Taste and add more cayenne if desired. Serve hot.

For a great quick dinner, pair this substantial and deeply flavorful soup with a big salad. Chickpeas, also known as garbanzo beans, are one of the easiest beans to digest. They're also a good source of protein, fiber, and iron. In this recipe, half of the chickpeas are blended to create an appealing creamy texture.

MEDITERRANEAN chickpea soup

MAKES 4 SERVINGS

2 tablespoons extra-virgin olive oil

2 cups water, plus more as needed

½ cup chopped onion

½ red bell pepper, finely diced

1 clove garlic, minced

3 cups cooked or canned chickpeas, liquid reserved

1 cup bean cooking liquid, vegetable broth (preferably homemade, page 78), **water, or a combination**

1 can (6 ounces) **tomato paste, or ½ cup tomato sauce**

3 tablespoons chopped green olives

1 teaspoon salt

½ teaspoon dried oregano

1 bay leaf

1. Put 1 tablespoon of the oil, 1 cup of the water, and the onion, bell pepper, and garlic in a soup pot over medium heat. Cook, stirring frequently, until the onion is translucent, about 10 minutes.

2. Put 1½ cups of the chickpeas and the bean cooking liquid in a blender or food processor and process until smooth.

3. Pour the mixture into the soup pot. Stir in the remaining 1½ cups of chickpeas, the remaining cup of water, and the tomato paste, olives, salt, oregano, and bay leaf.

4. Cover and simmer, stirring occasionally, for 1 hour, adding more water if needed to maintain a thick but soupy consistency.

5. Stir in the remaining tablespoon of oil just before serving. Serve hot.

6. Stored in a sealed container, Mediterranean Chickpea Soup will keep for 3 days in the refrigerator or 3 months in the freezer.

This scrumptious and substantial Mediterranean soup can easily serve as a complete meal. The pesto, which is stirred in just before serving, is an unconventional version that incorporates tomato paste and has a slightly chunky texture.

PESTO-INFUSED bean and vegetable soup

MAKES 8 SERVINGS

10 cups water

1½ cups scrubbed and diced carrots

1½ cups diced leeks (see note, page 75) or onions

1½ cups scrubbed and diced potatoes

1½ cups cut green beans, in 1-inch pieces

1½ cups cooked or canned kidney beans

½ cup broken spaghetti

1 slice stale whole-grain bread, crumbled

1 teaspoon salt

½ teaspoon ground pepper

1 can (6 ounces) tomato paste

¼ cup chopped fresh basil leaves, lightly packed, or 1½ tablespoons dried

¼ cup extra-virgin olive oil

¼ cup Nut Parmesan (page 122)

4 cloves garlic, minced

1. Put the water, carrots, leeks, and potatoes in a large soup pot and bring to a boil over high heat. Decrease the heat to medium-low, cover, and simmer, stirring occasionally, for 30 minutes.

2. Stir in the green beans, kidney beans, spaghetti, bread, salt, and pepper. Cover and simmer, stirring occasionally, until all the vegetables are tender, about 15 minutes.

3. To make the pesto, put the tomato paste, basil, oil, Nut Parmesan, and garlic in a medium bowl and whisk until well combined.

4. Stir the pesto into the soup just before serving. Serve hot.

5. Stored in a sealed container in the refrigerator, Pesto-Infused Bean and Vegetable Soup will keep for 3 days.

This nourishing soup features the rich, nutty flavor and appealing chewy texture of barley. A combination of Indian spices adds a subtle yet interesting flavor and also aids in digestion of the lentils.

barley and red LENTIL SOUP

MAKES 4 TO 6 SERVINGS

1 tablespoon extra-virgin olive oil

4 cups water or vegetable broth (preferably homemade, page 78)

1 cup chopped onion or leek (see note, page 75)

1 stalk celery, chopped

1 tablespoon minced garlic

1 tablespoon peeled and grated fresh ginger

¾ teaspoon ground coriander

¾ teaspoon ground cumin

¾ teaspoon ground turmeric

Pinch cayenne

½ cup hulled barley, soaked in water for 4 to 8 hours (see note)

½ cup red lentils, soaked in water for 8 hours

1½ cups chopped baby spinach, lightly packed

1 cup scrubbed and chopped carrots

1 large tomato, chopped, or 1 can (14 ounces) **diced tomatoes, with juice**

¼ cup chopped fresh parsley

2 bay leaves

1 teaspoon salt

1. Put the oil, ½ cup of the water, and the onion, celery, garlic, and ginger in a soup pot over medium heat. Cook, stirring frequently, until the vegetables begin to soften, about 5 minutes.

2. Stir in the coriander, cumin, turmeric, and cayenne and cook for 3 minutes, stirring frequently.

3. Drain and rinse the barley and lentils. Add them to the soup pot, along with the remaining 3½ cups of water and the spinach, carrots, tomato, parsley, and bay leaves. Decrease the heat to medium-low, cover, and simmer, stirring occasionally, until the lentils are tender, about 30 minutes.

4. Stir in the salt. Remove the bay leaves before serving. Serve hot.

5. Stored in a sealed container, Barley and Red Lentil Soup will keep for 3 days in the refrigerator or 3 months in the freezer.

NOTE: The barley and lentils can be soaked together.

CHAPTER 8

Salads

This salad is delightful at the beginning of the summer when the first garden vegetables are ready to enjoy.

summer salad WITH HERBS AND GARDEN VEGETABLES

MAKES 4 TO 6 SERVINGS

6 tablespoons Simple Oil and Vinegar Dressing (page 116)

2 heads Boston or butter lettuce, washed and spun dry

2 carrots, scrubbed and grated

4 baby English cucumbers, sliced

1 cup fresh green peas

6 radishes, sliced

½ cup chopped fresh parsley

½ cup chopped fresh chives

¼ cup hempseeds

1. Put the dressing in a large salad bowl.
2. Add the lettuce, carrots, cucumbers, peas, radishes, parsley, chives, and hempseeds and toss until well combined. Serve immediately.

Grated beets give this satisfying salad a creamy pink hue.

SUMPTUOUS caesar salad

MAKES 4 SERVINGS

⅔ cup Vegan Caesar Salad Dressing (page 119)

2 romaine lettuce hearts, sliced

2 cups sprouts (such as alfalfa, clover, lentil, sunflower, or a combination)

⅔ English cucumber, halved lengthwise and sliced

1 cup scrubbed and grated beet

½ cup thinly sliced red onion

¼ cup hempseeds

1. Put the dressing in a large salad bowl.
2. Add the lettuce, sprouts, cucumber, beet, onion, and hempseeds, and toss until well combined. Serve immediately.

This lovely salad livens up mixed baby lettuces and beautifully accents holiday meals and winter gatherings.

winter salad WITH FIGS AND NUTS

6 tablespoons Balsamic Vinaigrette (page 117)

½ cup thinly sliced fennel bulb

¼ cup chopped dried Black Mission figs

¼ cup chopped walnuts, pecans, or brazil nuts

¼ cup thinly sliced red onion

5 pitted green olives, chopped

1 teaspoon chopped fresh thyme, or ½ teaspoon dried

6 cups mixed baby greens

1. Put the vinaigrette in a medium salad bowl.

2. Add the fennel, figs, walnuts, onion, olives, and thyme and stir until well combined. Let sit at room temperature for up to 1 hour.

3. Add the baby greens and toss until well combined. Serve immediately.

Winter Salad with Apricots and Nuts: Replace the figs with chopped dried apricots.

Enjoy the earthy flavors in this simple, beautiful salad—and know that you're doing your body a big favor. Carrots are one of the richest sources of the antioxidant beta-carotene, which benefits virtually every organ of the body, including the liver, lungs, kidneys, spleen, pancreas, intestine, and skin.

CARROT-BEET salad

MAKES 4 TO 6 SERVINGS

¼ cup chopped fresh dill, or
2 teaspoons dried dill weed

2 tablespoons cider vinegar or freshly squeezed lemon juice

1 tablespoon extra-virgin olive oil

1 tablespoon hempseed or flaxseed oil

½ teaspoon salt

2½ cups scrubbed and grated carrots (about 3 carrots)

1½ cups scrubbed and grated beet (about 1 large beet)

1 apple with peel, grated

2 inches daikon radish, scrubbed and grated

1. Put the dill, vinegar, olive oil, hempseed oil, and salt in a medium serving bowl and whisk until well blended.

2. Add the carrots, beet, apple, and daikon and toss gently until well combined. Let sit at room temperature for up to 1 hour before serving. Serve at room temperature or chilled.

3. Stored in a sealed container in the refrigerator, Carrot-Beet Salad will keep for 3 days.

NOTE: You can make this salad in a jiffy if you use a food processor fitted with the grating blade to prepare the carrots, beet, apple, and daikon.

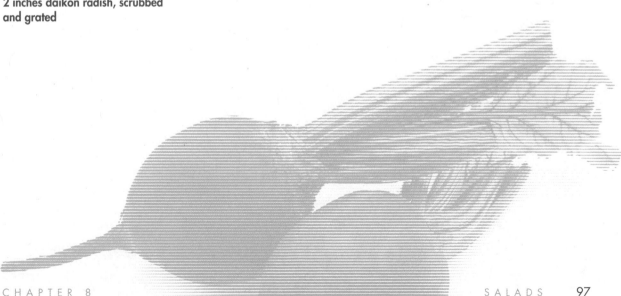

This lively salad brings together three classic autumn flavors: fennel, apple, and walnuts. It is beautiful, crunchy, and savory, with just a touch of sweetness provided by the apples.

apple-fennel SALAD

MAKES 4 TO 6 SERVINGS

2½ tablespoons extra-virgin olive oil

2 tablespoons freshly squeezed lemon juice

2 teaspoons grated lemon zest

2 teaspoons chopped fresh thyme, or 1 teaspoon dried

¾ teaspoon salt

2 cups julienned fennel (about 1 small fennel bulb; see note)

2 cups julienned apples with peel (about 3 apples)

⅛ teaspoon ground pepper (optional)

½ cup coarsely chopped walnuts

1. Put the oil, lemon juice, lemon zest, thyme, and salt in a medium serving bowl and whisk until well blended.

2. Add the fennel and apples and toss until evenly coated. Let sit at room temperature for up to 2 hours for the flavors to meld.

3. Season with the optional pepper and toss gently until evenly distributed. Scatter the walnuts over the top. Serve at room temperature or chilled.

4. Stored in a sealed container in the refrigerator, Apple-Fennel Salad will keep for 2 days.

NOTE: To prepare the fennel, first remove the stalks with a knife. Save these for use in fresh juice, such as Fennel Ambrosia (page 62). Thinly slice the bulb from top to bottom, then thinly cut the slices from top to bottom to create matchsticks. To prepare the apples, cut them in half and remove the core. Thinly slice each half from top to bottom, then thinly cut the slices from top to bottom to create matchsticks.

This is a great way to prepare raw kale, which is highly nutritious but too tough or intensely flavored for some people. These qualities disappear when the kale is massaged with the other ingredients in this salad, leaving it soft and coated in complementary flavors.

KALE-AVOCADO salad

MAKES 4 SERVINGS

5 cups stemmed and thinly sliced kale, lightly packed

1 avocado, cubed (see note, page 67)

1½ tablespoons freshly squeezed lemon juice

1 teaspoon salt

1 tomato, chopped

¼ cup chopped raw almonds or Brazil nuts

1 green onion, thinly sliced

1. Put the kale, avocado, lemon juice, and salt in a medium serving bowl. Massage the ingredients together by hand until the avocado is creamy and the kale is wilted.

2. Stir in the tomato, almonds, and green onion. Serve immediately.

NOTE: To strip the leaves off the kale stem, simply hold the base of the stem in one hand, grasp the bottom of the leaf where it attaches to the stem with the other hand, and pull upward along the stem.

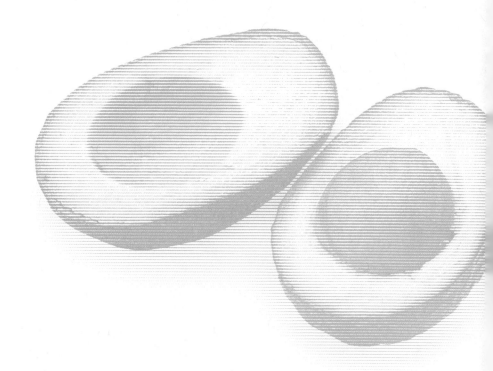

Unlike many salads, this one improves as it sits; because the vegetables are dense, they benefit from having time to marinate and soften in the dressing. Kale is such a nourishing green, and this is an extremely pleasing way to enjoy it. Make this salad when mandarin oranges are abundantly available, typically November through January.

SWEET KALE salad

MAKES 4 SERVINGS

½ cup freshly squeezed orange juice (about 1 orange), or juice of 3 mandarin oranges

¼ cup extra-virgin olive oil

2 tablespoons cider vinegar

1 tablespoon maple syrup

½ teaspoon salt

5 cups stemmed and thinly sliced kale, lightly packed

3 mandarin oranges, separated into segments and segments cut in half; 1 pear, sliced; or 6 fresh figs, quartered

1 small carrot, scrubbed and grated

½ cup thinly sliced fennel

½ cup finely chopped red cabbage

¼ cup thinly sliced red onion

¼ cup chopped raw almonds, pecans, or walnuts

3 tablespoons dried cranberries, raisins, or dried blueberries

1. Put the juice, oil, vinegar, maple syrup, and salt in a large serving bowl and whisk until well blended.

2. Add the kale, mandarin oranges, carrot, fennel, cabbage, and onion and toss gently until well combined. Let sit at room temperature for 30 to 60 minutes.

3. Just before serving, add the almonds and cranberries and toss gently to combine.

4. Stored in a sealed container in the refrigerator, Sweet Kale Salad will keep for 3 days.

This salad is basic fare but very special in its own right, thanks to a well-rounded combination of six key flavors: sweetness from carrot, maple syrup, and raisins; sourness from apple and vinegar; saltiness from celery and salt; bitterness from cabbage and parsley; astringency from apple, cabbage, and walnuts; and pungency from onion and cabbage.

cabbage salad WITH APPLE, PECANS, AND RAISINS

See photo facing page 83.

MAKES 4 TO 6 SERVINGS

2 tablespoons cider vinegar

1½ tablespoons extra-virgin olive oil

1½ tablespoons hempseed oil, flaxseed oil, or additional olive oil

1 tablespoon maple syrup

1 teaspoon salt

½ teaspoon ground fennel

2 cups finely chopped green cabbage

¾ cup finely chopped red cabbage

1 apple with peel, finely diced

1 carrot, scrubbed, quartered lengthwise, and thinly sliced

1 stalk celery, thinly sliced

½ cup chopped fresh parsley

½ cup chopped pecans or walnuts

½ cup raisins

¼ cup thinly sliced sweet or red onion

1. Put the vinegar, olive oil, hempseed oil, maple syrup, salt, and ground fennel in a medium serving bowl and whisk until well blended.

2. Add the green cabbage, red cabbage, apple, carrot, celery, parsley, pecans, raisins, and onion and toss until well combined. Serve at room temperature or chilled.

3. Stored in a sealed container in the refrigerator, Cabbage Salad with Apple, Pecans, and Raisins will keep for 3 days.

Broccoli Salad with Apple, Pecans, and Raisins: Replace all or part of the cabbage with an equal amount of finely chopped broccoli florets and tender stems.

Rich in bone-strengthening silicon, beets improve circulation, purify the blood, strengthen the heart, and benefit the liver. This salad is particularly delicious from midsummer to early fall, when beets with their greens are readily available and at the height of their season.

beets and greens WITH LEMON-BASIL DRESSING

12 small or 6 medium beets with greens (see note)

¼ cup extra-virgin olive oil

3 tablespoons freshly squeezed lemon juice

1 tablespoon balsamic vinegar

½ teaspoon salt

½ cup fresh basil leaves, lightly packed and thinly sliced

1. Cut the greens from the beets. Scrub the beets well. Wash the greens in a generous amount of cold water. Cut the leaves crosswise into 1-inch-wide strips and cut the stems into ½-inch lengths.

2. Put 1 inch of water in a medium saucepan. Add the beets and bring to a boil over high heat. Decrease the heat to medium-low, cover, and cook until fork-tender, between 15 and 30 minutes depending on the size of the beets. Drain well.

3. Put 1 inch of water in a separate medium saucepan. Add the beet greens and stems and bring to a boil over high heat. Decrease the heat to medium-high, cover, and cook until tender, 5 to 10 minutes. Let cool, then drain and squeeze out any excess moisture.

4. Drain the beets and cool them quickly in cold water. When they are cool enough to handle, slip off their skins by hand. Halve the beets, then slice them crosswise.

5. Put the oil, lemon juice, vinegar, and salt in a medium serving bowl and whisk until well blended.

6. Add the beets and greens and stir gently until evenly coated.

7. Just before serving, stir in the basil. Serve warm, at room temperature, or chilled.

8. Stored in a sealed container in the refrigerator, Beets and Greens with Lemon-Basil Dressing will keep for 3 days.

NOTE: If beet greens aren't available, substitute 4 cups of chopped spinach or Swiss chard, lightly packed.

This fresh and healthful version of a classic is a particularly good choice when new potatoes arrive at markets at the height of summer.

POTATO salad

1½ pounds new red or white potatoes, scrubbed and cut into 1-inch cubes

½ cup vegan mayonnaise

¼ cup chopped fresh parsley

¼ cup chopped fresh dill, or 2 teaspoons dried dill weed

1 tablespoon Dijon mustard

½ teaspoon salt

1 carrot, scrubbed, quartered lengthwise, and thinly sliced

2 stalks celery with leaves, halved lengthwise and thinly sliced

1 cup raw fresh or thawed frozen peas

3 tablespoons finely chopped green or red onion

Paprika, for garnish

1. Steam the potatoes over medium heat until fork-tender, 15 to 20 minutes. Let cool.

2. Put the vegan mayonnaise, parsley, dill, mustard, and salt in a medium serving bowl and stir until well combined.

3. Add the carrot, celery, peas, green onion, and potatoes and stir gently until well combined. Garnish with a sprinkling of paprika if desired. Serve at room temperature or chilled.

4. Stored in a sealed container in the refrigerator, Potato Salad will keep for 3 days.

Potato Salad with Avocado Dressing: Replace the vegan mayonnaise with 1 large avocado blended with 2 tablespoons of freshly squeezed lemon juice and 2 tablespoons of water. Taste the salad before serving and add more salt if desired.

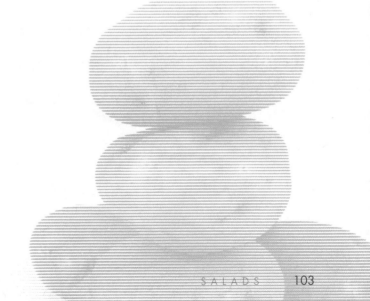

Make this savory salad in the springtime when the first edible greens of the season, fiddlehead ferns and wild leeks, may be available at your local farmers' market. If you can't find those ingredients, though, you can still enjoy this salad and even make it year-round by replacing the fiddleheads with broccoli and the leeks with red onion, as in the variation that follows.

wild rice AND FIDDLEHEAD SALAD

MAKES 4 SERVINGS

¾ cup wild rice, soaked in water for 4 to 8 hours (see note)

2¼ cups water

3 cups young fiddleheads, trimmed and cleaned

3 tablespoons extra-virgin olive oil

2 tablespoons freshly squeezed lemon juice

1 tablespoon grated lemon zest

1 teaspoon maple syrup

1 teaspoon Dijon mustard

½ teaspoon salt

1 carrot, scrubbed and grated

½ cup chopped fresh parsley

⅓ cup thinly sliced wild leeks or red onion

½ cup chopped walnuts, raw almonds, or pecans

1. Drain the wild rice in a strainer and rinse thoroughly. Transfer to a medium saucepan, add the water, and bring to a boil over high heat. Decrease the heat to medium-low, cover, and cook for 40 minutes, until the grains open and curl. Drain and let cool.

2. Meanwhile, put 2 inches of water in a medium saucepan. Add the fiddleheads and bring to a boil over high heat. Decrease the heat to medium-low, cover, and cook until tender, about 8 minutes. Drain and run under cold water to cool.

3. Put the oil, lemon juice, lemon zest, maple syrup, mustard, and salt in a medium serving bowl and whisk until well blended.

4. Add the carrot, parsley, leeks, rice, and fiddleheads and stir gently until well combined.

5. Just before serving, stir in the walnuts. Serve at room temperature or chilled.

6. Stored in a sealed container in the refrigerator, Wild Rice and Fiddlehead Salad will keep for 3 days.

NOTE: Soaking the wild rice will make it more digestible and speed the cooking time, but if need be, you can skip that step.

Wild Rice and Broccoli Salad: Substitute 3 cups of broccoli florets for the fiddleheads. The broccoli may be cooked in the same was as the fiddleheads, but decrease the cooking time to just 4 minutes. Alternatively, you can steam the broccoli until tender-crisp if you prefer.

This flavorful salad, which features both raw and cooked ingredients, is so substantial that it can serve as a meal in itself. Soba is a type of Japanese noodle made from buckwheat, which is high in protein; 100 percent buckwheat varieties are gluten-free.

soba noodle salad WITH BABY BOK CHOY

MAKES 2 MAIN-DISH SERVINGS OR 4 SIDE-DISH SERVINGS

6 ounces soba noodles

3 tablespoons cold-pressed sesame oil

1½ tablespoons cider vinegar

1 tablespoon reduced-sodium tamari

1 tablespoon maple syrup

1 teaspoon minced garlic

1 teaspoon peeled and grated fresh ginger

¼ teaspoon ground cinnamon

¼ teaspoon ground cumin

4 cups thinly sliced baby bok choy

1 cup mung bean sprouts or lentil sprouts (optional)

1 carrot, scrubbed and grated

1 large stalk celery, thinly sliced diagonally

2 radishes, halved and thinly sliced (optional)

2 green onions, thinly sliced

¼ cup coarsely chopped raw almonds or cashews

Gomasio (preferably homemade, page 122; optional)

1. Bring a large pot of water to a boil over high heat. Stir in the soba and return to a boil. Decrease the heat to medium-low and cook, stirring occasionally, until tender but firm, 5 to 8 minutes. (The time will vary depending on the variety of soba.) Drain in a colander and rinse under cold water.

2. Put the oil, vinegar, tamari, maple syrup, garlic, ginger, cinnamon, and cumin in a medium serving bowl and whisk until well blended.

3. Add the bok choy, optional sprouts, carrot, celery, optional radishes, green onions, and almonds. Stir gently until well combined. Add the soba and toss gently to combine.

4. Just before serving, sprinkle with gomasio if desired. Serve at room temperature or chilled.

5. Stored in a sealed container in the refrigerator, Soba Salad with Baby Bok Choy will keep for 3 days.

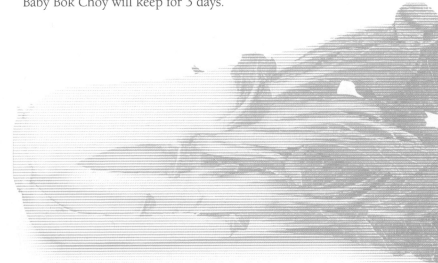

Thanks to the chickpeas and optional tofu cottage cheese, this delightful pasta salad is substantial enough to serve as a main dish.

GREEK pasta salad

MAKES 4 MAIN-DISH SERVINGS OR 6 SIDE-DISH SERVINGS

8 ounces brown rice pasta spirals or other shaped pasta

3 tablespoons extra-virgin olive oil

3 tablespoons freshly squeezed lemon juice

1 tablespoon chopped fresh dill, or 1 teaspoon dried dill weed

1 tablespoon chopped fresh oregano, or 1 teaspoon dried

1 teaspoon salt

1 teaspoon minced garlic

1½ cups cooked or canned chickpeas, rinsed if canned

2 tomatoes, diced

¾ cup Tofu Cottage Cheese (page 72) **or crumbled firm tofu** (optional)

½ English cucumber, peeled and diced

1 red or yellow bell pepper, diced

½ cup sliced green or black olives

1 stalk celery, thinly sliced

2 green onions, thinly sliced

1. Bring a large pot of water to a boil over high heat. Add the pasta and return to a boil. Decrease the heat to medium-low and cook, stirring occasionally, until tender but firm, 9 to 10 minutes. Drain in a colander and rinse under cold water.

2. Put the oil, lemon juice, dill, oregano, salt, and garlic in a large serving bowl and whisk until well mixed.

3. Add the chickpeas, tomatoes, optional Tofu Cottage Cheese, cucumber, bell pepper, olives, celery, green onions, and pasta. Toss gently until well combined. Serve at room temperature or chilled.

4. Stored in a sealed container in the refrigerator, Greek Pasta Salad will keep for 3 days.

NOTE: Rice pasta, an excellent gluten-free option to conventional pasta, is readily available at natural food stores and supermarkets. Be sure to rinse the drained pasta under cold running water. Otherwise it will be sticky.

This classic protein- and fiber-rich salad is perfect for taking to a potluck. If you have leftovers, serve them with freshly pressed juice or a tossed green salad and corn on the cob for a satisfying meal.

five-bean SALAD

MAKES 12 SIDE-DISH SERVINGS

¼ cup extra-virgin olive oil

¼ cup cider vinegar

¼ cup unrefined cane sugar

1½ teaspoons salt

1 pound green beans, cut into 1-inch pieces

1½ cups cooked or canned lima beans, rinsed if canned

1½ cups cooked or canned red kidney beans, rinsed if canned

1½ cups cooked or canned pinto beans, rinsed if canned

1½ cups cooked or canned chickpeas, rinsed if canned

1 cup finely chopped red or Vidalia onion

1 red or yellow bell pepper, finely chopped

1. Put the oil, vinegar, sugar, and salt in a small saucepan and gently warm over medium-low heat, stirring occasionally, until the sugar is dissolved.

2. Put 1 inch of water in a medium saucepan. Add the green beans and bring to a boil over high heat. Decrease the heat to medium-high, cover, and cook until tender-crisp, about 4 minutes. Drain and rinse under cold water.

3. Put the oil mixture, green beans, lima beans, kidney beans, pinto beans, chickpeas, onion, and bell pepper in a large serving bowl and stir until well combined.

4. For optimum flavor, cover and refrigerate for 8 to 12 hours before serving. Serve chilled or at room temperature.

5. Stored in a sealed container in the refrigerator, Five-Bean Salad will keep for 5 days.

This salad brings out the best in lentils, which have been sustaining people for thousands of years. Like all legumes, they are inexpensive but extremely nutritious, filling, and flavorful. This dish keeps well, so take any leftovers to school or work for lunch the next day. Serve it with a green salad and seasonal vegetables for a complete meal.

LENTIL salad

MAKES 4 SIDE-DISH SERVINGS

1 cup French or brown lentils, soaked in water for 8 hours

4 cups water

2 cloves garlic, peeled

2 teaspoons chopped fresh thyme, or 1 teaspoon dried

2 bay leaves

¼ cup extra-virgin olive oil

3 tablespoons cider vinegar or freshly squeezed lemon juice

1 teaspoon ground fennel

1 teaspoon Dijon mustard

¾ teaspoon salt

⅛ teaspoon ground pepper

½ cup diced celery

½ cup diced red or yellow bell pepper (optional)

½ cup chopped fresh parsley

¼ cup finely chopped red onion

1. Drain and rinse the lentils. Transfer to a medium pot and add the water, garlic, thyme, and bay leaves. Bring to a boil over high heat. Decrease the heat to medium, cover partially, and cook, stirring occasionally, until the lentils are tender but firm, about 20 minutes.

2. Drain and rinse the lentils and discard the bay leaves. Remove the garlic cloves and put them in a medium serving bowl. Set the lentils aside to cool.

3. Mash the garlic with a fork. Add the oil, vinegar, fennel, mustard, salt, and pepper and whisk until well blended.

4. Add the celery, bell pepper, parsley, onion, and lentils and stir until well combined. Serve at room temperature.

5. Stored in a sealed container in the refrigerator, Lentil Salad will keep for 3 days.

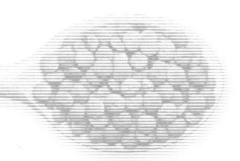

This Asian-style meal in a bowl may become one of your favorite dishes. It's simple yet thoroughly pleasing to all of the senses, with interesting flavors, vibrant colors, and a variety of textures and shapes. To speed preparation at mealtime, you can cook the tofu and quinoa earlier in the day.

asian quinoa AND TOFU SALAD

1½ tablespoons reduced-sodium tamari

1 tablespoon cold-pressed sesame oil

1½ cups water

8 ounces firm tofu, cut into ½-inch cubes

¾ cup quinoa, soaked in water for 4 to 8 hours (see note)

½ cup Asian Dressing (page 118)

4 cups sliced romaine lettuce

½ English cucumber, peeled, halved lengthwise, and sliced

½ red or yellow bell pepper, sliced

½ cup thinly sliced red cabbage

1 carrot, scrubbed and grated

3 green onions, thinly sliced

3 small radishes, halved and thinly sliced (optional)

⅓ cup coarsely chopped raw almonds or cashews

1. Preheat the oven to 350 degrees F.
2. Put the tamari, oil, and ¼ cup of the water in a 13 x 9-inch baking pan and whisk until well blended. Add the tofu and gently turn or stir until evenly coated. Bake for 20 to 25 minutes, stirring once after 10 minutes, until lightly browned and crispy. Let cool to room temperature.
3. Meanwhile, drain and rinse the quinoa in a fine-mesh strainer. Transfer a medium saucepan and add the remaining 1¼ cups of water. Bring to a boil over high heat. Decrease the heat to medium-low, cover, and cook undisturbed for 15 to 20 minutes, until the water is absorbed and the quinoa is tender. Let stand, covered, for 5 minutes, then uncover and let cool to room temperature.
4. Put the dressing in a large serving bowl. Add the lettuce, cucumber, bell pepper, cabbage, carrot, green onions, and optional radishes and toss until well combined.
5. Add the tofu and quinoa and stir gently until well combined. Sprinkle the chopped almonds over the top. Serve immediately.

NOTES

- If you don't have time to soak the quinoa, increase the amount of water for cooking the quinoa to 1½ cups.
- Because the romaine lettuce wilts, this salad is best served right after it has been made. If there is too much salad for one meal, add the dressing only to the portion that will be eaten right away.

For a complete meal, serve this filling dish with a tossed green salad.

rice and bean salad WITH CASHEWS

¾ cup brown rice, soaked in water for 4 to 8 hours (see note)

1¼ cups water

3 tablespoons extra-virgin olive oil

2 tablespoons freshly squeezed lemon juice

1 tablespoon reduced-sodium tamari

1 tablespoon chopped fresh oregano, or 1 teaspoon dried

1 teaspoon minced garlic

1½ cups cooked or canned red kidney beans or chickpeas, rinsed if canned

2 stalks celery, finely chopped

½ cup raw cashews, coarsely chopped

3 green onions, thinly sliced

¼ cup chopped fresh parsley

1. Drain and rinse the rice. Transfer to a medium saucepan. Add the water and bring to a boil over high heat. Decrease the heat to medium-low, cover, and cook undisturbed for 35 to 40 minutes, until the water is absorbed and the rice is tender. Let stand, covered, for 5 minutes, then uncover and let cool to room temperature.

2. Put the oil, lemon juice, tamari, oregano, and garlic in a medium serving bowl and whisk until well blended.

3. Add the rice, beans, celery, cashews, green onions, and parsley and stir until well combined. Serve at room temperature.

4. Stored in a sealed container in the refrigerator, Rice and Bean Salad with Cashews will keep for 1 day (any longer than that and the rice may get hard).

Quinoa and Black Bean Salad with Cashews: For a pleasing alternative, use 2 cups of cooked quinoa (see page 182) in place of the rice and cooked black beans instead of kidney beans or chickpeas.

NOTES

- If you don't have time to soak the rice, increase the amount of water to 1½ cups.
- Although this salad is a good the next day, you may want to stir in a splash of lemon juice to brighten the flavors.

CHAPTER 9

Sauces, Salad Dressings, and Savory Sprinkles

This tart and tangy sauce looks and tastes amazing with holiday meals.

FRESH cranberry relish

2 cups fresh or frozen cranberries

2 apples with peel, cut into large chunks

1 orange with peel, quartered, seeded and chopped

¼ cup maple syrup, plus more as needed

1. Put the cranberries, apples, and orange in a food processor and pulse until finely chopped.
2. Add the maple syrup and pulse to combine. Taste and add more maple syrup if desired.
3. Stored in a sealed container in the refrigerator, Fresh Cranberry Relish will keep for 5 days.

Use this tasty sauce on Marinated Vegetable and Tofu Kabobs (page 130). Or for a simple and pleasing main dish, put tofu or tempeh slices in a baking pan, cover with the sauce, and bake at 350 degrees F for thirty minutes, or until golden.

teriyaki SAUCE

⅓ cup reduced-sodium tamari

2 tablespoons water

2 tablespoons freshly squeezed lemon juice

1 tablespoon maple syrup

1 tablespoon cold-pressed sesame oil

2 teaspoons peeled and grated fresh ginger

1 teaspoon minced garlic

1. Put all the ingredients in a jar with a tight-fitting lid and shake to combine.
2. Stored in a sealed container in the refrigerator, Teriyaki Sauce will keep for 1 week.

This savory sauce is wonderful over vegetables, patties, or loaves, including Root Fries (page 160), Eggplant-Pecan Patties (page 131), Millet-Rice Patties (page 132), or Cashew-Carrot Loaf (page 133).

creamy tamari GRAVY

MAKES 2½ CUPS

2 tablespoons extra-virgin olive oil

¼ cup spelt flour or whole wheat flour

2 cups water

3 tablespoons reduced-sodium tamari, plus more as needed

1. Heat the oil in a medium saucepan over medium heat.

2. Gradually add the flour, stirring constantly until smooth and lump-free. Cook, stirring constantly, for 1 minute.

3. Switch to a whisk and gradually add the water, about ½ cup at a time, whisking constantly until smooth. Decrease the heat to medium-low and simmer, stirring frequently, until thick, about 8 minutes.

4. Stir in the tamari. Taste and add more tamari if desired. Serve hot.

5. Stored in a sealed container in the refrigerator, Creamy Tamari Gravy will keep for 4 days. Warm it gently over low heat before serving.

NOTE: If the gravy sits for a while, it will thicken. To thin it, stir in a little water or plain, unsweetened nondairy milk, 1 tablespoon at a time, to achieve the desired consistency.

Mushroom-Leek Gravy: Put the oil, ¼ cup of water, 1 cup of sliced cremini or other mushrooms, and 1 cup of sliced leek in a medium skillet over medium heat. Cook, stirring occasionally, until the vegetables are tender and lightly browned, about 8 minutes. Add the flour, stir until evenly distributed, and proceed with step 3.

This gravy is the perfect topping for the Macrobiotic Bowl (page 127). Or simply pour it over brown rice and steamed vegetables. Delicious!

MISO gravy

1½ tablespoons dark miso

2 cups water

1½ tablespoons cold-pressed sesame oil

1 cup chopped leek (see note, page 75) or onion

3 tablespoons spelt flour or whole-wheat flour

½ teaspoon dried thyme

1 tablespoon reduced-sodium tamari

1. Put the miso and ¼ cup of the water in a small cup and stir to form a smooth paste.

2. Put the oil, ¼ cup of the water, and the leek in a medium saucepan over medium heat. Cook and stir until tender, about 5 minutes.

3. Gradually add the flour, stirring constantly until evenly distributed. Stir in the thyme.

4. Switch to a whisk and gradually add the remaining 1½ cups of water, ½ cup at a time, whisking constantly until smooth. Decrease the heat to medium-low and simmer, stirring frequently, until thick, about 5 minutes.

5. Stir in the tamari. Remove from the heat and stir in the miso mixture. Serve immediately.

6. Stored in a sealed container in the refrigerator, Miso Gravy will keep for 4 days. Warm it gently over low heat before serving.

This sauce tastes incredibly like cheese. For a child-friendly main dish, try it with noodles, as in Vegan Macaroni and Cheese with Broccoli (page 138). For more sophisticated fare, use it in Cheesy Vegetable Pie (page 136).

CHEESY sauce

MAKES 3 CUPS

1½ cups raw cashews, soaked in water for 4 hours (see note, page 68)

2 cups water

3 tablespoons nutritional yeast

2 tablespoons freshly squeezed lemon juice

1 tablespoon chopped onion

1 small clove garlic, chopped

¾ teaspoon salt

1. Drain and rinse the cashews. Transfer to a blender.
2. Add the water, nutritional yeast, lemon juice, onion, garlic, and salt and process until completely smooth, stopping occasionally to scrape down the blender jar with a rubber spatula and move the mixture toward the blades.
3. Stored in a sealed container in the refrigerator, Cheesy Sauce will keep for 3 days. To use the sauce as a topping for noodles, potatoes, or grains, transfer to a medium saucepan and warm gently over low heat before serving.

Cheddar Cheesy Sauce: Add ⅓ red bell pepper, coarsely chopped, before blending.

Use a two-to-one ratio of oil to vinegar, as here, to create a light, simple dressing for any salad. This one is particularly delightful at the height of summer on fresh, local greens and vegetables.

simple oil and vinegar DRESSING

MAKES ¾ CUP

½ cup extra-virgin olive oil

¼ cup cider vinegar

½ teaspoon salt

1. Put all the ingredients in a jar with a tight-fitting lid and shake to combine.
2. Stored in a sealed jar in the refrigerator, Simple Oil and Vinegar Dressing will keep for 1 week.

NOTE: For basic salad dressings that are simply whisked, like most vinaigrettes, you can streamline preparation and cleanup by making the dressing right in the salad bowl. Just put the dressing ingredients in the salad bowl and whisk them together. Then all you have to do is add the salad ingredients and toss! You will likely need to decrease the quantity of the individual ingredients—just make sure you keep the proportions the same.

This is an easy, pleasing dressing that uses some of the excellent high-quality cold-pressed oils available these days. Try it on a salad made with leaf lettuce and seasonal vegetables of your choice, along with sprouts for added nutrition.

balsamic VINAIGRETTE

MAKES ¾ CUP

¼ cup balsamic vinegar

3 tablespoons flaxseed or hempseed oil

3 tablespoons extra-virgin olive oil

2 tablespoons maple syrup

½ teaspoon salt

1. Put all the ingredients in a jar with a tight-fitting lid and shake to combine.
2. Stored in a sealed jar in the refrigerator, Balsamic Vinaigrette will keep for 1 week.

This is a delightful recipe for a classic dressing.

LEMON vinaigrette

MAKES ⅔ CUP

⅓ cup extra-virgin olive oil

1½ tablespoons cider vinegar

1½ tablespoons freshly squeezed lemon juice

1 tablespoon chopped fresh herbs (such as tarragon or thyme), or ½ teaspoon dried

1 tablespoon maple syrup

1 teaspoon Dijon mustard

½ teaspoon salt

Ground pepper

1. Put the oil, vinegar, lemon juice, herbs, maple syrup, mustard, and salt in a jar with a tight-fitting lid and shake to combine.
2. Season with pepper to taste and shake again. Stored in a sealed jar in the refrigerator, Lemon Vinaigrette will keep for 1 week.

Use this tasty dressing on salads for a delightfully different flavor. Consider putting an Asian twist on the other salad ingredients too, by including bok choy, broccoli, cauliflower, celery, napa cabbage, shiitake mushrooms, or even sea vegetables, baked tofu, or cold cooked rice or noodles.

asian DRESSING

MAKES ⅔ CUP

3 tablespoons rice vinegar or cider vinegar

3 tablespoons cold-pressed sesame oil

2 tablespoons reduced-sodium tamari

1½ tablespoons maple syrup

1 teaspoon minced garlic

1 teaspoon peeled and grated fresh ginger

1. Put all the ingredients in a jar with a tight-fitting lid and shake to combine.

2. Stored in a sealed jar in the refrigerator, Asian Dressing will keep for 1 week.

Use this zippy dressing on chopped romaine hearts, as in a traditional caeser salad, or try it over raw or steamed vegetables.

VEGAN caesar salad dressing

MAKES 1¼ CUPS

⅓ cup extra-virgin olive oil

¼ cup cider vinegar

¼ cup water

3 tablespoons freshly squeezed lemon juice

2 tablespoons raw almond butter

2 teaspoons minced garlic

1 teaspoon Dijon mustard

1 teaspoon maple syrup

½ teaspoon salt

1. Put all the ingredients in a glass jar or bowl and whisk to combine. Alternatively, process with a hand blender.
2. Stored in a sealed jar in the refrigerator, Vegan Caesar Salad Dressing will keep for 1 week.

Be sure to use a mild, light miso, sometimes called mellow miso. Darker miso has too strong a flavor for this bright and creamy dressing.

DIJON-MISO dressing

⅓ cup extra-virgin olive oil

¼ cup freshly squeezed lemon juice
(about 1 large lemon)

3 tablespoons light miso

3 tablespoons water

2 teaspoons Dijon mustard

1 teaspoon minced garlic

1. Put all the ingredients in a glass jar or bowl and whisk to combine. Alternatively, process with a hand blender.
2. Stored in a sealed jar in the refrigerator, Dijon-Miso Dressing will keep for 1 week.

Sweet Dijon-Miso Dressing: Add 1 tablespoon of maple syrup.

This versatile dressing with no added oils is delicious over any garden salad. For optimum freshness and flavor, the dressing should be used immediately, so you'll want to make it at a time when you're serving a big salad.

avocado DRESSING

1 avocado

1 tomato

1 small stalk celery, or ½ red bell pepper

2 tablespoons freshly squeezed lemon juice

½ teaspoon salt

1. Put all the ingredients in a blender and process until smooth.
2. Alternatively, process with a hand blender. Use immediately.

For a classic Greek salad, toss this dressing with a mix of romaine lettuce, cucumbers, tomatoes, bell peppers, red onion, and Greek olives.

greek salad DRESSING

MAKES 1½ CUPS

½ cup extra-virgin olive oil

¼ cup freshly squeezed lemon juice
(about 1 large lemon)

¼ cup water

1 tomato

2 tablespoons chopped red or sweet onion

2 tablespoons tofu

4 large basil leaves, or ½ teaspoon dried basil

1 teaspoon Dijon mustard

1 teaspoon balsamic or cider vinegar

½ teaspoon salt

1. Put all the ingredients in a blender and process until smooth.
2. Stored in a sealed jar in the refrigerator, Greek Salad Dressing will keep for 1 week.

Gomasio, a calcium-rich topping made of ground sesame seeds and salt, can be sprinkled on steamed vegetables, salads, and Asian-style soups for a nutty flavor. It looks especially appealing when made with a combination of white and black sesame seeds. Because seeds tend to go rancid more quickly once they're ground, make this in small batches to keep it fresh.

gomasio

MAKES ¼ CUP

¼ cup raw white or black sesame seeds or a combination

1 teaspoon salt

1. Put the sesame seeds and salt in a coffee grinder or blender and process until most of the seeds are broken open.
2. Stored in a sealed jar in the refrigerator, Gomasio will keep for 1 month.

Keep this cheesy-tasting topping in the refrigerator at all times to complement Italian-style dishes.

nut PARMESAN

MAKES ½ CUP

½ cup raw cashews

1½ tablespoons nutritional yeast

½ teaspoon salt

1. Put all the ingredients in a coffee grinder or blender and pulse until the mixture has the texture of coarse meal.
2. Stored in a sealed jar in the refrigerator, Nut Parmesan will keep for 1 month.

VARIATION: Use ¼ cup of raw Brazil nuts, macadamia nuts, pine nuts, or almonds in place of ¼ cup of the cashews.

CHAPTER 10

Main Dishes

This rich, hearty stew is excellent fall and winter fare. It's also a great way to use up vegetables that may be languishing in the refrigerator. Plus, any leftovers taste wonderful the next day.

WARMING vegetable stew

MAKES 4 TO 6 SERVINGS

2 tablespoons extra-virgin olive oil

2¼ cups water or vegetable broth (preferably homemade, page 78), plus more as needed

1 onion, chopped

1 leek, sliced (see note, page 75), or 1 additional onion, chopped

1 cup sliced cabbage, or 1½ cups halved Brussels sprouts

10 cremini or button mushrooms, quartered

1 large clove garlic, minced

3 tablespoons spelt flour or whole wheat flour

4 medium red or Yukon Gold potatoes, scrubbed and diced

2 carrots, scrubbed, halved lengthwise, and thickly sliced

1½ cups diced fresh or canned tomatoes (one 14-ounce can, with juice)

1½ cups cooked or canned kidney beans, rinsed if canned

1½ cups cooked or canned lima beans, rinsed if canned

¼ cup chopped fresh parsley

2 tablespoons reduced-sodium tamari

1 teaspoon salt

¼ teaspoon dried basil

¼ teaspoon dried oregano

¼ teaspoon dried thyme

2 bay leaves

Ground pepper

1. Put the oil, ¼ cup of the water, and the onion, leek, cabbage, mushrooms, and garlic in a soup pot over medium heat. Cook, stirring frequently, until the vegetables begin to soften, about 5 minutes.

2. Gradually add the flour, stirring constantly until the vegetables are coated. Increase the heat to medium-high and gradually add the remaining 2 cups of water, ½ cup at a time, stirring constantly, until thickened.

3. Stir in the potatoes, carrots, tomatoes, kidney beans, lima beans, parsley, tamari, salt, basil, oregano, thyme, and bay leaves. Add just enough water to barely cover the vegetables. Decrease the heat to medium-low, cover, and simmer, stirring occasionally, until the vegetables are tender and the flavors have blended, about 1 hour.

4. Season with pepper to taste. Serve hot.

NOTE: When a recipe calls for tomatoes, depending on the season, it may be a better choice nutritionally and economically to use canned tomatoes. If you're fortunate, perhaps you can find locally grown tomatoes in cans or jars. Sometimes local organic farms preserve ripe tomatoes at the peak of the season and make them available at nearby stores. The flavor of such tomatoes is often superior to fresh tomatoes that are imported or grown in greenhouses.

Variation: Add 2 or 3 quartered ears of corn or 1 cup of peeled and diced yam or winter squash when adding the potatoes.

These delectable baked beans are surrounded by a sweet, dark golden-brown sauce. To help with digestion, keep the meal simple by serving Maple Baked Beans with a green salad and steamed seasonal vegetables.

maple BAKED BEANS

6 cups cooked or canned navy beans, liquid reserved

1 onion, finely chopped

⅓ cup fruit-sweetened ketchup

¼ cup blackstrap molasses

¼ cup maple syrup

3 tablespoons reduced-sodium tamari

2 tablespoons extra-virgin olive oil

1 tablespoon dry mustard

1 teaspoon salt

Water, as needed

1. Preheat the oven to 325 degrees F.
2. Drain the beans, reserving the liquid. Transfer the beans to a 2-quart casserole dish.
3. Add the onion, ketchup, molasses, maple syrup, tamari, oil, mustard, salt, and enough bean liquid or water to barely cover the beans. Stir to combine.
4. Cover and bake for 2 to 3 hours, adding more bean liquid or water as needed to keep the beans just covered. The beans should be coated by a dark golden-brown sauce. Taste and add more salt, tamari, or maple syrup if desired. Serve hot.

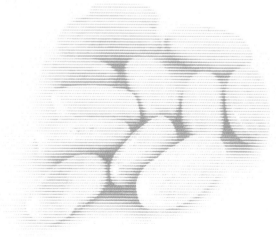

This cold-weather meal, which consists of cooked millet, navy bean stew, and steamed vegetables smothered in Miso Gravy, is guaranteed to satisfy.

MACROBIOTIC bowl

MAKES 4 SERVINGS

1½ cups millet, soaked in water for 4 to 8 hours (see note)

2¾ cups water

3 cups cooked or canned navy beans, liquid reserved

1 cup bean cooking liquid, vegetable broth (preferably homemade, page 78), **or water, as needed**

1 onion, diced

1 carrot, scrubbed, halved lengthwise, and sliced diagonally

1 stalk celery, halved lengthwise and sliced diagonally

½ cup chopped fresh parsley

1 teaspoon salt

4 cups stemmed and coarsely chopped green or black kale, lightly packed

2 cups peeled and cubed sweet potatoes (about 2 small sweet potatoes)

2 cups Miso Gravy (page 114)

4 tablespoons gomasio (preferably homemade, page 122)

1. Drain and rinse the millet. Transfer to a medium saucepan. Add the water and bring to a boil over high heat. Decrease the heat to medium-low, cover, and cook undisturbed for 40 minutes, until the water is absorbed and the millet is tender. Let stand, covered, for 5 minutes.

2. Meanwhile, put the navy beans, bean cooking liquid, onion, carrot, celery, parsley, and salt in a medium saucepan over medium-low heat and stir to combine. Cover, and simmer, stirring occasionally, until the vegetables are very soft, about 40 minutes. Add more bean cooking liquid as needed to prevent sticking.

3. Put 1 inch of water in a medium pot. Add the kale and sweet potatoes and bring to a boil over high heat. Decrease the heat to medium-low, cover, and cook until tender, about 15 minutes. Drain well.

4. To serve, divide the millet among four soup bowls. Top with the kale and sweet potatoes and put the beans on the side. Drizzle with the gravy and sprinkle with the gomasio. Serve immediately.

NOTE: If you don't have time to soak the millet, increase the amount of water to 3 cups.

What a blessing this dish is when time is short and you want to have a meal that's satisfying, tantalizing, and kind to the digestive system. Don't let the simplicity of this recipe trick you into thinking the results are plain and uninteresting. The variety of toppings make it truly exceptional.

go-to grain AND VEGETABLE BOWL

MAKES 2 SERVINGS

1 cup rice blend, soaked in water for 4 to 8 hours (see notes)

1½ cups water

1 leek, halved lengthwise and sliced (see note, page 75)

2 carrots, scrubbed, halved lengthwise, and sliced

2 cups chopped cauliflower

2 heads baby bok choy, sliced

1 cup mung bean, lentil, or other sprouts

¼ cup chopped raw almonds or Brazil nuts

¼ cup chopped fresh cilantro, chives, or parsley

Fermented vegetables (such as kimchi or sauerkraut)

Gomasio (preferably homemade, page 122)

Salt or seasoned salt

Cold-pressed sesame oil

1. Drain and rinse the rice. Transfer to a medium saucepan. Add the water and bring to a boil over high heat. Decrease the heat to medium-low, cover, and cook undisturbed for 35 to 40 minutes, until the water is absorbed and the rice is tender. Let stand, covered, for 5 minutes.

2. Meanwhile, put 1 inch of water in a medium saucepan. Add the leek, carrots, cauliflower, and bok choy, layering them in that order, and bring to a boil over high heat. Decrease the heat to medium-low, cover, and simmer until all the vegetables are tender, about 15 minutes. Drain well. (For an alternative cooking method, see the notes.)

3. Put the sprouts, almonds, and cilantro in separate small bowls on the table. Pass fermented vegetables, gomasio, salt, and sesame oil at the table.

4. To serve, divide the rice between two large soup bowls and top with the cooked vegetables. Serve immediately, letting each person season his or her bowl as desired.

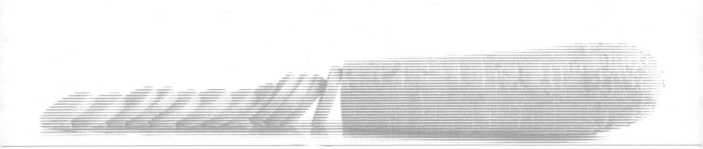

NOTES

- If you don't have time to soak the rice, increase the amount of water to 2 cups.
- Rice blends are available packaged at natural food stores, or you can create your own using a combination of brown rice, wild rice, red rice, and black rice.
- If you have a tiered vegetable steamer that allows you to cook the rice in the bottom pot and steam the vegetables on top, start steaming the vegetables 10 minutes after the rice has begun cooking. This will save energy, and the juices from the vegetables will flavor the rice.

Variations

- Replace the rice with millet or quinoa. Quinoa cooks more quickly than rice or millet, so be sure to start cooking the vegetables right after you get the quinoa going.
- Different vegetables can be substituted freely in this dish, depending on your taste and what's in season, or just for variety. When substituting vegetables, try to include one orange vegetable (such as winter squash or yams) and one leafy green (such as collard greens, kale, or Swiss chard) for optimum nutrition and visual appeal. When cooking the vegetables, layer them with denser vegetables at the bottom and more tender vegetables at the top.
- Use different nuts, herbs, and cold-pressed oils to create endless variations.

These kabobs are perfect barbecue fare. Serve them over steamed quinoa, with corn on the cob and a big green salad on the side.

MARINATED vegetable and tofu kabobs

MAKES 4 SERVINGS

⅔ cup Teriyaki Sauce (page 112)

1 pound firm or extra-firm tofu, cubed

1 zucchini, halved lengthwise and sliced ½ inch thick

16 cremini or button mushrooms, halved

16 cherry tomatoes

1 red bell pepper, cut into large squares

1 yellow bell pepper, cut into large squares

½ red onion, cut into large squares, layers separated

1. Put the Teriyaki Sauce in a 13 x 9-inch baking pan. Add the tofu, zucchini, mushrooms, cherry tomatoes, bell peppers, and onion and stir gently until evenly coated. Marinate for 1 to 4 hours at room temperature, gently stirring a time or two.

2. Heat a grill on medium-low. Soak 4 bamboo skewers in water for about 15 minutes.

3. Drain the tofu and vegetables and reserve the marinade. Thread the tofu and vegetables on the skewers, alternating them and arranging the pieces tightly, so they touch.

4. Grill for 10 to 15 minutes, until the vegetables are tender and the tofu is browned. As the kabobs cook, occasionally turn them and brush with the reserved marinade.

5. Serve hot, drizzled with any remaining marinade.

Most people wouldn't guess there's eggplant in these enticing, savory patties. For a complete menu featuring them, check out the holiday menu on page 196.

eggplant-pecan PATTIES

8 cups diced eggplant with peel
(about 1 large eggplant)

⅔ cup pecans

¾ cup old-fashioned rolled oats

1 slice whole-grain bread, torn into several large pieces

⅓ cup chopped celery

1 tablespoon reduced-sodium tamari

1½ teaspoons dried sage

½ teaspoon salt

1. Preheat the oven to 350 degrees F.
2. Lightly oil a baking sheet.
3. Put 1 inch of water in a large saucepan. Add the eggplant and bring to a boil over high heat. Decrease the heat to medium-low, cover, and simmer for 15 minutes, until the eggplant is tender.
4. Drain well. Return the eggplant to the saucepan and mash it with a potato masher or large fork.
5. Put the pecans in a food processor and process until finely ground. Add the oats, bread, and celery and process until coarsely ground. Don't overprocess; the mixture should retain some texture.
6. Add the pecan mixture to the eggplant, along with the tamari, sage, and salt. Mix thoroughly with your hands. Let stand for 5 minutes.
7. Taste and add more tamari, sage, or salt if desired. Form the mixture into 8 to 12 patties and place them on the prepared baking sheet.
8. Bake for 25 minutes, until firm and crisp, turning the patties over halfway through the baking time. Serve hot.

Millet is a nutty-tasting, easy-to-digest, gluten-free cereal grain that is rich in B vitamins and minerals. For a meal that's sure to appease the heartiest appetites, serve these patties with Creamy Tamari Gravy (page 113), mashed or roasted potatoes, steamed seasonal vegetables, and a big salad. They're also great stuffed into pita bread along with lettuce or sprouts, tomatoes, pickles, ketchup, mustard, and other condiments. Be sure to use short-grain brown rice here; it's stickier than long-grain brown rice and helps the patties hold together.

millet-rice PATTIES

MAKES 10 TO 12 PATTIES (4 TO 8 SERVINGS)

½ cup millet, soaked in water for 4 to 8 hours (see notes)

½ cup short-grain brown rice, soaked in water for 4 to 8 hours

2 cups water

½ cup raw sunflower seeds

8 ounces firm tofu, crumbled

1 cup scrubbed and grated carrots

1 cup fresh breadcrumbs or coarsely ground old-fashioned rolled oats

½ cup finely chopped onion or leek (see note, page 75)

3 tablespoons extra-virgin olive oil

1 tablespoon nutritional yeast flakes

1 tablespoon reduced-sodium tamari

2 teaspoons dried dill weed

1 teaspoon dried thyme

1 teaspoon dried sage

½ teaspoon salt

¼ cup spelt flour or additional breadcrumbs or coarsely ground rolled oats, if needed

1. Drain and rinse the millet and rice. Transfer to a medium saucepan. Add the water and bring to a boil over high heat. Decrease the heat to medium-low, cover, and cook undisturbed for 40 minutes, until the water is absorbed and the grains are tender. Let stand, covered, for 5 minutes. Transfer to a large bowl and let cool.

2. Preheat the oven to 325 degrees F.

3. Lightly oil a baking sheet.

4. Put the sunflower seeds in a blender or coffee grinder and process until finely ground. Transfer to the bowl with the cooled grains.

5. Add the tofu, carrots, breadcrumbs, onion, oil, nutritional yeast, tamari, dill weed, thyme, sage, and salt and mix thoroughly with your hands, squeezing to break up the grains. Let sit for about 5 minutes.

6. Squeeze the mixture to test whether it holds together. If it doesn't, add the flour, 1 tablespoon at a time, until it does, thoroughly mixing it in with your hands after each addition.

7. Form the mixture into patties, making sure that they are fairly flat; otherwise they may fall apart when turned over during baking. Place the patties on the prepared baking sheet.

8. Bake for 15 minutes. Carefully turn the patties over and cook for 10 minutes longer, until the surface is firm and crisp. Serve hot.

NOTES

- The millet and rice can be soaked together.
- If you don't have time to soak the grains, increase the amount of water to 2½ cups.

This savory loaf is ideal for holidays and celebrations. It's excellent served with Creamy Tamari Gravy (page 113), roasted potatoes or Root Fries (page 160), seasonal vegetables, and a big green salad.

CASHEW-CARROT loaf

MAKES 8 SERVINGS

6 cups scrubbed and chopped carrots (about 2½ pounds)

2 cups raw cashews

1 cup finely chopped leek (see note, page 75) **or mild onion**

1 cup finely chopped celery

½ cup whole wheat flour, spelt flour, or oat flour

2 tablespoons extra-virgin olive oil

2 teaspoons dried sage, crushed

1 teaspoon salt

1 teaspoon dried basil

½ teaspoon dried thyme

½ teaspoon ground pepper

1. Preheat the oven to 350 degrees F.
2. Lightly oil an 8-inch square baking pan.
3. Put 2 inches of water in a medium saucepan. Add the carrots and bring to a boil over high heat. Decrease the heat to medium-low, cover, and simmer until tender, 10 to 15 minutes.
4. Drain and mash with a fork or potato masher until fairly smooth or transfer to a food processor and process until fairly smooth. Transfer to a large bowl.
5. Put the cashews in a food processor or blender and process until finely ground. Transfer to the bowl with the carrots.
6. Add the leek, celery, flour, oil, sage, salt, basil, thyme, and pepper and stir until thoroughly combined.
7. Transfer the mixture to the prepared pan and pat it into an even layer.
8. Bake for 40 minutes, until the edges begin to look dry. Let sit for 10 minutes before cutting. Serve hot.

This version of Shepherd's Pie makes use of three protein-rich gluten-free grains, which are artfully seasoned and used as the bottom layer of the pie. Creamy Tamari Gravy (page 113) is a must to serve with it.

shepherd's PIE

MAKES 8 SERVINGS

½ cup millet, soaked in water for 4 to 8 hours (see notes)

3 cups water

1½ teaspoons salt

½ cup quinoa, soaked in water for 4 to 8 hours

½ cup buckwheat groats, soaked in water for 4 to 8 hours

8 medium gold or russet potatoes, peeled and quartered

3 tablespoons extra-virgin olive oil

Plain, unsweetened nondairy milk, as needed

2 tablespoons reduced-sodium tamari

1 teaspoon minced garlic

1 teaspoon ground coriander

1 teaspoon dried thyme

½ teaspoon dried sage

¼ teaspoon dried savory

1½ cups sliced leeks (see note, page 75) or onions

1½ cups thawed frozen corn kernels

2½ cups Creamy Tamari Gravy (page 113)

1. Drain and rinse the millet. Transfer to a medium saucepan. Add 2¾ cups of the water and ½ teaspoon of the salt and bring to a boil over high heat. Decrease the heat to medium-low, cover, and cook undisturbed for 25 minutes, until the millet has opened up and the liquid is creamy.

2. Drain and rinse the quinoa and buckwheat in a fine-mesh strainer. Stir them into the millet, cover, and cook undisturbed for 20 to 25 minutes, until the water is absorbed and the grains are tender. Let stand, covered, for 5 minutes, then uncover and let cool to room temperature.

3. Meanwhile, to make the mashed potatoes, put 3 inches of water in a medium saucepan. Add the potatoes and bring to a boil over high heat. Decrease the heat to medium-low, cover, and simmer until fork-tender, about 20 minutes.

4. Drain, reserving the cooking liquid. Add 2 tablespoons of the oil and the remaining teaspoon of salt to the potatoes. Mash with a potato masher or large fork, adding as much potato cooking liquid or nondairy milk as needed to create a creamy, smooth texture. (Any remaining potato cooking liquid can be used in the gravy.)

5. Preheat the oven to 350 degrees F.

6. Oil a 13 x 9-inch baking pan.

7. Add the tamari, garlic, coriander, thyme, sage, and savory to the cooled grains. Mix thoroughly with your hands, squeezing to break up the grains. Taste and add more salt or herbs as desired.

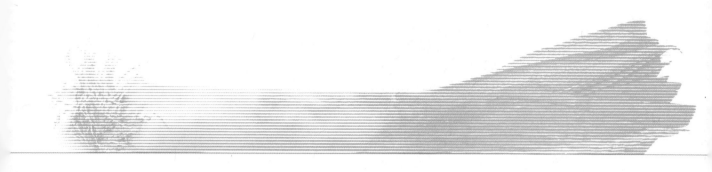

8. Put the remaining tablespoon of oil, the remaining ¼ cup of water, and the leeks in a skillet over medium heat. Cover and cook, stirring occasionally, until the leeks are tender, about 10 minutes. Stir in the corn, cover, and cook, stirring frequently, for 5 minutes.

9. To assemble the pie, transfer the grain mixture to the prepared pan and pat it into an even layer. Spread the leeks and corn evenly over the grain mixture. Top with the mashed potatoes, spreading them evenly over the top.

10. Bake for 40 minutes, until golden brown. Serve hot, passing the Creamy Tamari Gravy at the table.

NOTES

- You can soak the quinoa and buckwheat together, but be sure to soak the millet separately, as it's cooked separately for a while before the quinoa and buckwheat are added.

- If you don't have time to soak the grains, increase the amount of water for cooking them to 3 cups.

Variation: Substitute sweet potatoes for the potatoes.

With its quinoa and chickpea crust, this hearty, gluten-free meal in a pan is packed with vegetable protein. Leftovers are superb the next day for lunch. It's also well suited to experimentation. Vary the grains, legumes, vegetables, sauces, and herbs each time you make it to create your own variations. They are bound to be delightful.

CHEESY vegetable pie

MAKES 4 TO 6 SERVINGS

¾ cup quinoa, soaked in water for 4 to 8 hours (see note)

1⅓ cups water

1½ cups cooked or canned chickpeas, rinsed if canned

3 tablespoons extra-virgin olive oil

1 teaspoon dried oregano

½ teaspoon salt

¼ cup spelt flour or other flour, as needed

6 tablespoons Lemony Tomato Tapenade (page 69)

2 cups coarsely chopped spinach or Swiss chard, lightly packed

1 zucchini, grated

1 small sweet potato, peeled and grated

1 cup thinly sliced leek (see note, page 75) or onion

1 cup finely chopped cauliflower (optional)

3 cups Cheesy Sauce or Cheddar Cheesy Sauce (page 115)

1 large or 2 small tomatoes, thinly sliced (optional)

1. Drain and rinse the quinoa in a fine-mesh strainer. Transfer to a small saucepan. Add the water and bring to a boil over high heat. Decrease the heat to medium-low, cover, and cook undisturbed for 15 to 20 minutes, until the water is absorbed and the quinoa is tender. Let stand, covered, for 5 minutes.

2. Preheat the oven to 325 degrees F.

3. Oil a 13 x 9-inch baking pan.

4. To make the crust, put the quinoa, chickpeas, oil, oregano, and salt in a food processor and process until smooth. The dough should be thick and sticky. If it seems too thin, add the flour, 1 tablespoon at a time, processing after each addition. Add more flour as needed until the mixture is thick.

5. Transfer the dough to the prepared pan and press it into an even layer.

6. Spread the tapenade over the dough in an even layer.

7. Put the spinach, zucchini, sweet potato, leek, and optional cauliflower in a medium bowl. Add the Cheesy Sauce and stir until the vegetables are evenly coated.

8. Distribute the vegetable mixture evenly over the tapenade. Top with the optional tomatoes, distributing them in an even layer.

9. Cover and bake for 25 minutes. Uncover and bake for 20 minutes longer, until firm and lightly browned. Let sit for 10 minutes. Serve hot.

NOTE: If you don't have time to soak the quinoa, increase the amount of water to 1½ cups.

Variations

- Replace the cooked quinoa with 2 cups of cooked rice or millet.
- Replace the chickpeas with cooked lentils, white kidney beans, or navy beans.
- Replace the tapenade with homemade or store-bought pesto.
- Vary the vegetables depending on what's in season or what you have on hand.

This recipe may well become one of your favorite "fast foods."

vegan macaroni and cheese WITH BROCCOLI

MAKES 4 SMALL SERVINGS

10 ounces brown rice elbow macaroni or other whole-grain shaped pasta

4 cups chopped broccoli

1½ cups Cheesy Sauce or Cheddar Cheesy Sauce (page 115)**, plus more as needed**

1. Bring a large pot of water to a boil over high heat. Stir in the macaroni and return to a boil. Decrease the heat to medium-low and cook, stirring occasionally, until tender but firm. Drain and rinse under cold water.

2. Put 1 inch of water in a medium saucepan. Add the broccoli and bring to a boil over high heat. Decrease the heat to medium, cover, and cook until tender, about 5 minutes. Drain and return to the pot.

3. Gently stir in the macaroni and Cheesy Sauce. Cook over medium heat, stirring gently from time to time, until heated through, about 5 minutes. Serve hot.

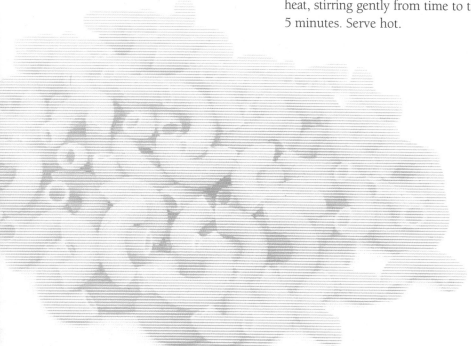

The vegetable-laden Italian-style sauce in this recipe is splendid over any kind of pasta.

PASTA WITH chunky tomato sauce

MAKES 6 TO 8 SERVINGS

5 cups fresh or canned diced tomatoes (three 14-ounce cans, with juice)

3 cups crushed or strained tomatoes (about two 14-ounce cans)

2 onions, chopped

8 ounces cremini or white button mushrooms, sliced

2 small green or yellow zucchini, halved lengthwise and sliced 1 inch thick

2 carrots, scrubbed, halved lengthwise, and thinly sliced

2 stalks celery, halved lengthwise and thinly sliced

1 red bell pepper, diced

3 tablespoons reduced-sodium tamari

2 tablespoons unrefined cane sugar

1 tablespoon minced garlic

1 teaspoon salt

1 teaspoon dried basil

½ teaspoon dried oregano

¼ teaspoon dried thyme

2 bay leaves

1 pound whole-grain pasta

2 tablespoons extra-virgin olive oil

Nut Parmesan (page 122), **for garnish**

1. Put the diced tomatoes, crushed tomatoes, onions, mushrooms, zucchini, carrots, celery, bell pepper, tamari, sugar, garlic, salt, basil, oregano, thyme, and bay leaves in a large pot. Bring to a boil over high heat. Decrease the heat to medium-low and simmer uncovered, stirring occasionally, for 1½ hours.

2. Bring a large pot of water to a boil over high heat. Stir in the pasta and return to a boil. Decrease the heat to medium-low and cook, stirring occasionally, until tender but firm. Drain and rinse under cold water.

3. Stir the oil into the sauce. Ladle the sauce over the pasta and serve immediately, sprinkled with Nut Parmesan.

Variation: Serve the sauce over baked spaghetti squash instead of pasta. To prepare the squash, preheat the oven to 350 degrees F. Cut the squash in half lengthwise, scoop out the seeds, and put the halves cut-side down on a baking sheet. Bake for about 40 minutes, until tender. Cool slightly, then scrape the cooked squash out of the shell with a fork; the strands will resemble spaghetti.

This Italian peasant dish is wonderful served in big individual bowls with a fresh green salad on the side. Like many of the recipes in this book, this dish has all of the six flavors needed to fully nourish our bodies and our souls.

PASTA WITH beans and greens

MAKES 4 SERVINGS

12 ounces brown rice rotini or other whole-grain small pasta (such as elbow macaroni or fusilli)

2 tablespoons extra-virgin olive oil

¼ cup water

1½ cups diced onions or leeks (see note, page 75)

3 tablespoons minced garlic

5 cups chopped Swiss chard, spinach, or rapini

3 cups diced fresh or canned tomatoes (two 14-ounce cans, with juice)

1½ cups cooked or canned Roman beans or white kidney beans, rinsed if canned

1 teaspoon salt

1 teaspoon unrefined cane sugar

1 tablespoon freshly squeezed lemon juice

Nut Parmesan (page 122), **for garnish**

1. Bring a large pot of water to a boil over high heat. Stir in the pasta and return to a boil. Decrease the heat to medium-low and cook, stirring occasionally, until tender but firm. Drain and rinse under cold water.

2. Put 1 tablespoon of the oil and the water, onions, and garlic in a large skillet over medium heat. Cook, stirring frequently, for 5 minutes.

3. Stir in the chard. Decrease the heat to medium-low, cover, and cook, stirring occasionally, until the greens are wilted and tender, about 10 minutes.

4. Stir in the tomatoes, beans, salt, and sugar and simmer, stirring frequently, until heated through. Stir in the lemon juice and remaining tablespoon of oil just before serving.

5. To serve, divide the pasta among four individual bowls and ladle the vegetables over the top. Sprinkle with Nut Parmesan and serve immediately.

For a superb and well-balanced meal, pair these quick, vegetable-laden turnovers with a large green salad. They are also easy to adapt to special dietary needs, as sprouted grain wraps and gluten-free wraps work perfectly here. Leftovers are nicely portable, so pack them for school or work lunches the next day.

vegetable CALZONES

MAKES 4 CALZONES (4 SERVINGS)

2 cups chopped baby spinach, lightly packed

1 zucchini, grated

1 cup halved and sliced button or cremini mushrooms

½ cup thinly sliced red bell pepper

¼ cup chopped green or black olives (optional)

2 tablespoons nutritional yeast flakes (optional)

1½ tablespoons extra-virgin olive oil

1 teaspoon minced garlic

½ teaspoon salt

¼ teaspoon dried basil

¼ teaspoon dried oregano

4 whole-grain wraps

1 cup prepared pizza sauce or spaghetti sauce

1. Preheat the oven to 325 degrees F.
2. Combine the spinach, zucchini, mushrooms, bell pepper, optional olives, optional nutritional yeast, oil, garlic, salt, basil, and oregano in a large bowl.
3. Set two baking sheets on the counter. Place 2 wraps on each sheet. Spread ¼ cup of the pizza sauce evenly over each wrap, spreading it right to the edge.
4. Put one-fourth of the vegetable mixture in the center of each wrap. Spread the vegetables to within ½ inch of the edges.
5. Bake for 20 minutes, until the vegetables are tender and hot.
6. Use a spatula to fold each calzone over to enclose the vegetables. Let the calzones cool for 5 minutes before serving. For easier serving and eating, cut each calzone in half with a sharp knife. Serve hot or at room temperature.

This satisfying dish is always a hit. It's also perfect to contribute to a potluck.

bean enchiladas WITH RED SAUCE

MAKES 8 TO 10 LARGE ENCHILADAS (10 TO 20 SERVINGS)

5 tablespoons extra-virgin olive oil

¼ cup water

1 cup finely chopped onion

1 cup finely chopped red bell pepper

3 cups cooked or canned red kidney beans, liquid reserved

5 tablespoons chili powder

2 tablespoons freshly squeezed lemon juice

1½ teaspoon ground cumin

1½ teaspoons salt

¼ teaspoon cayenne, or ⅛ to ¼ teaspoon hot sauce

½ cup cornmeal

3 tablespoons spelt flour or whole wheat flour

3 cups crushed or strained tomatoes (about two 14-ounce cans)

8 to 10 whole-grain tortillas

2 cups Chunky Guacamole (page 67), for serving

1½ cups Tomato-Corn Salsa (page 68) or other salsa, for serving

½ cup chopped fresh cilantro, for serving

1. Preheat the oven to 325 degrees F.

2. Oil a 13 x 9-inch baking pan.

3. To make the filling, put 2 tablespoons of the oil and the water, onion, and bell pepper in a large skillet over medium heat. Cook, stirring frequently, until the vegetables are tender, about 6 minutes.

4. Add the beans, ¼ cup of the bean liquid or water, 3 tablespoons of the chili powder, the lemon juice and cumin, 1 teaspoon of the salt, and the cayenne.

5. To make the sauce, heat the remaining 3 tablespoons of oil in a medium saucepan over medium heat. Stir in the cornmeal, flour, remaining 2 tablespoons of chili powder, and remaining ½ teaspoon of salt. Cook and stir for 1 to 2 minutes. Stir in the tomatoes. Decrease the heat to medium low and simmer, stirring occasionally to prevent sticking, until thick, about 10 minutes. If the sauce gets too thick, add a little more bean liquid or water to maintain a pourable consistency.

6. Lay a tortilla flat on a work surface and put about ⅓ cup of the filling in a line across the middle of the tortilla. Roll up the tortilla around the filling and place it seam-side down in the prepared baking pan.

7. Pour the sauce over the enchiladas, distributing it evenly.

8. Bake for 20 to 25 minutes, until hot and bubbly.

9. Put the guacamole, salsa, and cilantro in separate small bowls on the table. Serve the enchiladas hot, cutting them in half for smaller appetites or large buffet tables. Let everyone season their serving as desired.

In this recipe, a flavorful chili is spooned over corn chips and fresh lettuce. Once you've made the chili, this dish couldn't be simpler to put together. Served topped with guacamole, salsa, and fresh herbs, it's a meal that's sure to please.

taco salad WITH CHILI

10 cups Zesty Bean Chili

1 bag (7 ounces) **baked corn chips** (4 to 6 cups)

1 romaine lettuce heart, sliced

2 cups Chunky Guacamole (page 67)

1½ cups Tomato-Corn Salsa (page 66) **or other salsa** (optional)

½ cup chopped fresh cilantro, for garnish

¼ cup sliced green onion, for garnish

1. For each serving, put a layer of corn chips on a dinner plate or in a shallow soup bowl. Add a layer of lettuce and ladle 1 heaping cup of chili over the lettuce. Top with a dollop of guacamole and a spoonful of salsa if desired.

2. Serve immediately, garnished with the cilantro and green onion.

With its curried rice, vegetables bathed in coconut milk, and sweet and crunchy toppings, this is a sublime and exotic dish.

sweet curried rice **AND VEGETABLES**

See photo facing page 146.

See photo facing page 146.

MAKES 6 SERVINGS

1½ cups brown basmati rice, soaked in water for 4 to 8 hours (see note)

3¾ cups water

2 teaspoons curry powder

2 teaspoons peeled and grated fresh ginger

1½ teaspoons salt

½ cup fresh basil leaves, lightly packed

2 tablespoons cold-pressed coconut oil

1½ cups sliced cremini or button mushrooms

1 red bell pepper, diced

2 teaspoons minced garlic

1 can (about 14 ounces) coconut milk

1 teaspoon salt

1 teaspoon chili sauce, plus more as desired

2 small sweet potatoes, peeled and sliced ½ inch thick (about 2 cups)

1½ cups diced fresh pineapple, or 1 apple, peeled and chopped

3 cups coarsely chopped spinach, lightly packed

1½ cups diced bananas, mangoes, or peaches, for serving

½ cup unsalted roasted peanuts or raw almonds, coarsely chopped, for serving

½ cup unsweetened shredded dried coconut, for serving

½ cup raisins, for serving

1. Drain and rinse the rice. Transfer to a medium saucepan. Add 2¾ cups of the water, the curry powder, 1 teaspoon of the ginger, and ½ teaspoon of the salt. Bring to a boil over high heat. Decrease the heat to medium-low, cover, and cook undisturbed for 35 to 40 minutes, until the water is absorbed and the rice is tender. Let stand, covered, for 5 minutes.

2. Set aside 5 of the basil leaves. Chop the remaining basil.

3. Put the oil, ¼ cup of the water, and the mushrooms, bell pepper, garlic, and remaining teaspoon of ginger in a large skillet over medium-high heat and cook, stirring frequently, for 5 minutes.

4. Stir in the coconut milk, the remaining ¾ cup of water, and the salt and chili sauce. Decrease the heat to medium and cook, stirring occasionally, until heated through, about 5 minutes.

5. Stir in the sweet potatoes and pineapple. Cover and cook, stirring occasionally, until the sweet potatoes are almost tender, about 10 minutes.

6. Stir in the spinach and chopped basil. Cover and cook, stirring occasionally, until the sweet potatoes are tender, about 6 minutes. Taste and add more chili sauce if desired.

7. Stack and roll up the reserved basil leaves lengthwise, then thinly slice them crosswise.

8. Put the bananas, peanuts, coconut, and raisins in separate small bowls on the table.

9. Transfer the rice to a large serving platter. Top with the vegetables and sprinkle the basil ribbons over the top. Serve hot, letting everyone garnish their serving as desired.

NOTE: If you don't have time to soak the rice, increase the amount of water for cooking the rice to 3 cups.

This dish is so simple—and so sublime.

cauliflower, spinach, and potatoes
IN MILD COCONUT CURRY

MAKES 4 SERVINGS

8 ounces potatoes (about 3 to 4 medium potatoes), **scrubbed and sliced ½ inch thick**

1 very small cauliflower, cut into small florets (about 3 cups)

1 can (about 14 ounces) **unsweetened coconut milk**

½ cup sliced green onions

½ cup chopped fresh cilantro

1 teaspoon salt

½ teaspoon ground turmeric

Dash chili sauce

1 tablespoon cold-pressed coconut oil

3 cups baby spinach, lightly packed

1. Put 1 inch of water in a large saucepan. Add the potatoes and bring to a boil over high heat. Decrease the heat to medium-low, cover, and cook for 5 minutes. Add the cauliflower and cook until the potatoes and cauliflower are tender, about 5 minutes. Drain well.

2. Put the coconut milk, ¼ cup of the green onions, 5 tablespoons of the cilantro, and the salt, turmeric, and chili sauce in a blender and process until smooth.

3. Put the coconut oil and remaining ¼ cup of green onions in a large skillet over medium-high heat. Cook and stir for 1 minute. Add the spinach and cook, stirring occasionally, until wilted and tender, about 5 minutes.

4. Pour the coconut milk mixture into the skillet. Add the potatoes and cauliflower and stir gently until well combined. Decrease the heat to medium-low, cover, and simmer, stirring occasionally, until heated through, about 5 minutes.

5. Serve hot, garnished with the remaining 3 tablespoons of cilantro.

Sweet Curried Rice and Vegetables, *pages 144–45*

Chocolate Mousse Pie, *page 172*

This is a flavorful but mildly spiced Indian-style stew that anyone can enjoy. Garam masala is a warming Indian spice blend; look for it at Indian food stores and well-stocked supermarkets. The blend of spices it contains can vary widely, so you might want to try several to find the variety you like best.

potato-cauliflower CURRY

MAKES 6 TO 8 SERVINGS

2 tablespoons cold-pressed coconut oil

1 teaspoon garam masala

½ teaspoon ground cumin

½ teaspoon ground turmeric

¼ teaspoon ground cardamom

¼ teaspoon cayenne

1 cup chopped leek (see note, page 75)

3 large red or Yukon Gold potatoes, scrubbed and diced (about 4½ cups)

1 small head cauliflower, cut into florets (about 4 cups)

1 can (about 14 ounces) unsweetened coconut milk

¾ teaspoon salt

1 cup water, as needed

1 cup diced fresh or canned tomatoes, with juice

1 cup cut green beans, in 1-inch pieces

½ cup chopped fresh cilantro (optional)

1. Heat the oil in a large pot over medium heat. Add the garam masala, cumin, turmeric, cardamom, and cayenne and cook, stirring constantly, until fragrant, about 1 minute, taking care not to burn the spices.

2. Stir in the leek and cook, stirring frequently, for 5 minutes. Stir in the potatoes and cauliflower and cook, stirring frequently, for 5 minutes.

3. Stir in the coconut milk and salt. Add the water, using just enough to barely cover the vegetables. Decrease the heat to medium-low, cover, and simmer, stirring occasionally, until the vegetables are almost tender, about 12 minutes.

4. Stir in the tomatoes, green beans, and optional cilantro. Cover and cook, stirring occasionally, until the green beans are tender, about 7 minutes. Serve hot.

Chickpea, Potato, and Cauliflower Curry: For a protein boost, add 1½ cups of cooked or canned chickpeas when you add the tomatoes.

This mildly spiced, simple East Indian stew is balancing and deeply nourishing. Mung beans are one of the easiest legumes to digest, and in this recipe they are presoaked along with the brown rice, making them even more digestible. If you have leftovers, they're even more flavorful the next day. Although traditional kitchari doesn't include vegetables, they enhance eye appeal, flavor, and nutrition, so I highly recommend adding the optional cauliflower, green beans, and potato.

kitchari

1 cup long-grain brown rice, soaked in water for 4 to 8 hours (see note)

½ cup whole mung beans, soaked in water for 8 hours

2 tablespoons cold-pressed coconut oil, plus more for serving

3¼ cups water, plus more as needed

1 large onion, halved and thinly sliced

1 tablespoon minced garlic

2 teaspoons peeled and grated fresh ginger

¾ teaspoon ground cinnamon

½ teaspoon ground cardamom

½ teaspoon ground turmeric

¼ teaspoon ground cloves

1½ cups diced fresh or canned tomatoes (one 14-ounce can, with juice)

¼ cup chopped fresh cilantro

8 fresh mint leaves, chopped

1 teaspoon salt

1½ cups chopped cauliflower (optional)

1 cup cut green beans, in 1-inch pieces (optional)

1 large potato, scrubbed and diced (optional)

1. Drain and rinse the rice and mung beans.
2. Put the oil, ¼ cup of the water, and the onion, garlic, ginger, cinnamon, cardamom, turmeric, and cloves in a large pot over medium heat. Cook, stirring frequently, for 6 minutes. Stir in the tomatoes, cilantro, and mint and cook, stirring frequently, for 3 minutes.
3. Stir in the rice, mung beans, salt, and remaining 3 cups of water. Decrease the heat to medium-low, cover, and simmer, stirring occasionally, for 40 minutes, adding water as needed to maintain a thick but soupy consistency.
4. Stir in the optional cauliflower, green beans, and potatoes. Cover and simmer, stirring occasionally, until the vegetables are tender and the rice is very soft, 8 to 10 minutes.
5. Serve hot, adding a teaspoon of coconut oil to each bowl if desired.

NOTE: You can soak the rice and mung beans together.

This elegant, flavorful dish can be varied by substituting whatever vegetables you have on hand.

quinoa and vegetables WITH THAI ALMOND SAUCE

3 tablespoons cold-pressed coconut oil

1 pound firm or extra-firm tofu, cubed

1½ cups red or white quinoa or a mixture, soaked in water for 4 to 8 hours (see note)

3¼ cups water, plus more as needed

1 cup freshly squeezed orange juice (about 2 oranges)

⅓ cup raw almond butter

3 tablespoons reduced-sodium tamari

2 teaspoons minced garlic

2 carrots, scrubbed and sliced

1 onion, diced

2 cups broccoli florets

1 cup thinly sliced green cabbage

1 cup thinly sliced red cabbage

1 red bell pepper, diced

1 cup snow peas, trimmed

4 green onions, sliced

½ cup chopped fresh cilantro, for garnish

1. Preheat the oven to 350 degrees F.

2. Put 1½ tablespoons of the oil in a 13 x 9-inch baking pan and put it in the oven for 3 minutes to melt the oil. Add the tofu and gently toss until evenly coated. Bake for about 25 minutes, until browned, gently stirring and turning the tofu halfway through the baking time.

3. Meanwhile, drain and rinse the quinoa in a fine-mesh strainer. Transfer to a small saucepan. Add 2½ cups of the water and bring to a boil over high heat. Decrease the heat to medium-low, cover, and cook undisturbed for 15 to 20 minutes. Let stand, covered, for 5 minutes.

4. To make the almond sauce, put the orange juice, ½ cup of the water, and the almond butter, tamari, and 1 teaspoon of the garlic in a bowl and whisk to combine. Alternatively, process with a hand blender. Add water if necessary to thin to a pourable consistency.

5. Put the remaining 1½ tablespoons of oil, the remaining ¼ cup of water, and the carrots, onion, and remaining teaspoon of garlic in a large skillet or wok over medium-high heat. Cook, stirring frequently, for 3 to 4 minutes. Add the broccoli and green and red cabbage and continue to cook and stir for 3 minutes. Add the bell pepper, snow peas, and green onions and cook, stirring frequently, for 2 minutes longer. Gently stir in the tofu.

6. To serve, divide the quinoa among individual plates. Spoon some of the vegetables and tofu over the top and drizzle with the almond sauce. Serve immediately, garnished with the cilantro.

NOTE: If you don't have time to soak the quinoa, increase the amount of water for cooking the quinoa to 3 cups.

Variation: Serve the vegetables, tofu, and sauce over cooked brown rice or Asian noodles instead of quinoa.

This stir-fry has tantalizing flavors and appealing bright colors. It's very versatile and can be a great way to use up extra vegetables you may have on hand.

SWEET-AND-SOUR tofu and vegetables

MAKES 4 SERVINGS

1 cup short-grain brown rice, soaked in water for 4 to 8 hours

2 cups water, plus more as needed

3½ tablespoons reduced-sodium tamari

2 tablespoons cold-pressed sesame oil

8 ounces firm tofu, cubed

½ cup freshly squeezed orange juice (about 1 orange)

2 tablespoons freshly squeezed lemon juice

2 tablespoons maple syrup

2 teaspoons peeled and grated fresh ginger

2 teaspoons arrowroot starch

1 onion, thinly sliced

1 zucchini, halved lengthwise and sliced ½ inch thick

1 large red bell pepper, sliced

1 carrot, scrubbed and sliced diagonally ¼ inch thick

¾ cup cut green beans, in 1-inch pieces

¾ cup cremini or button mushrooms, sliced

1 cup diced fresh pineapple

1. Drain and rinse the rice. Transfer to a medium saucepan. Add 1½ cups of the water and bring to a boil over high heat. Decrease the heat to medium-low, cover, and cook undisturbed for 35 minutes, until the water is absorbed and the rice is tender. Let stand, covered, for 5 minutes.

2. Preheat the oven to 350 degrees F.

3. Put ¼ cup of the water, 1½ tablespoons of the tamari, and 1 tablespoon of the oil in an 8-inch square baking pan. Whisk until well blended. Add the tofu and gently stir and turn until evenly coated. Bake for about 40 minutes, until the tofu is browned.

4. Put the orange juice, lemon juice, maple syrup, ginger, arrowroot starch, and remaining 2 tablespoons of tamari in a small bowl and whisk until well blended.

5. Put the remaining tablespoon of oil, the remaining ¼ cup of water, and the onion in a large skillet or wok over medium-high heat. Cook, stirring frequently, for 2 minutes. Add the zucchini, bell pepper, carrot, green beans, and mushrooms and cook, stirring frequently, until the vegetables are tender-crisp, 3 to 5 minutes, adding more water as needed to prevent sticking.

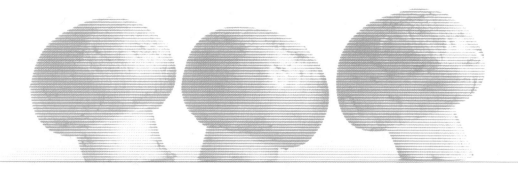

6. Decrease the heat to medium, stir in the orange juice mixture, and cook, stirring frequently, until the liquid thickens, about 2 minutes. Decrease the heat to medium-low and gently stir in the tofu and pineapple. Cook, stirring gently from time to time, until heated through, about 5 minutes.

7. To serve, divide the rice among four plates or bowls and top with the vegetable mixture. Serve immediately.

Variation: Omit the rice. Instead, cook 8 to 12 ounces of brown rice fettuccine or other whole-grain pasta in a large pot of boiling water until tender but firm. Drain and rinse under cold water. Add the vegetable mixture and toss gently until well combined.

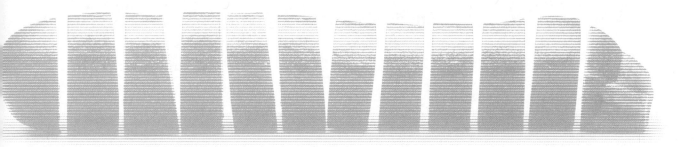

This is a delightful dish with layers of intriguing flavors and textures. Leftovers make an excellent packed lunch, as the flavors deepen over time and it is enjoyable at room temperature. Quinoa is used here, but any other grain or pasta will work perfectly well.

curried tofu WITH APRICOTS

1 cup red or white quinoa or a combination, soaked in water for 4 to 8 hours (see note)

1¾ cups water

¼ cup reduced-sodium tamari

1 green onion, chopped

2 tablespoons chopped fresh parsley

1½ tablespoons balsamic vinegar

1 tablespoon maple syrup

2 teaspoons raw white or black sesame seeds

2 teaspoons curry powder

1 teaspoon chili sauce, plus more as desired

1 pound extra-firm tofu, cubed

2 tablespoons cold-pressed coconut oil

1 onion, chopped

1 carrot, scrubbed and sliced diagonally

⅓ cup organic raw or unsalted dry-roasted peanuts or pecans, chopped

10 dried apricots, chopped

2 teaspoons minced garlic

1. Drain and rinse the quinoa in a fine-mesh strainer. Transfer to a medium saucepan. Add 1½ cups of the water and bring to a boil over high heat. Decrease the heat to medium-low, cover, and cook undisturbed for 15 to 20 minutes. Let stand, covered, for 5 minutes.

2. Put the tamari, green onion, parsley, balsamic vinegar, maple syrup, sesame seeds, curry powder, and chili sauce in a 13 x 9-inch baking pan. Whisk until well blended. Taste and add more chili sauce if desired. Add the tofu and gently stir and turn until evenly coated. Cover and let marinate for 1 to 4 hours at room temperature or up to 24 hours in the refrigerator, gently stirring a time or two as the tofu marinates.

3. Put the oil, the remaining ¼ cup of water, and the onion, carrot, peanuts, apricots, and garlic in a large skillet or wok over medium-high heat. Cook, stirring frequently, for 3 minutes. Decrease the heat to medium, cover, and cook, stirring occasionally, until the vegetables are almost tender, about 5 minutes.

4. Gently stir in the tofu and its marinade and cook, stirring gently from time to time, until the tofu begins to brown, about 10 minutes. Gently stir in the cooked quinoa. Serve hot.

NOTE: If you don't have time to soak the quinoa, increase the water for cooking the quinoa to 2 cups.

Side Dishes

Greens are a key element in a health-supporting plant-based diet, as they are rich in chlorophyll, vitamins, and minerals. Try to eat five servings of cooked greens per week. With this recipe, that should be easy to do. It transforms any type of greens into a tasty side dish.

GOOD greens

MAKES 4 SERVINGS

1 tablespoon extra-virgin olive oil or cold-pressed sesame oil

½ cup water, plus more as needed

1 onion or leek (see note, page 75), **sliced**

1 tablespoon minced garlic

8 cups stemmed and coarsely chopped leafy greens (such as kale, Swiss chard, spinach, rapini, mustard greens, or collards), **lightly packed**

¼ cup gomasio (preferably homemade, page 122; optional)

½ teaspoon salt (optional)

1. Put the oil, ¼ cup of the water, and the onion and garlic in a large skillet over medium heat. Cook, stirring frequently, for 5 minutes.

2. Add the greens and remaining ¼ cup of water and stir to combine. Decrease the heat to medium-low, cover, and cook, stirring occasionally, until tender, between 5 and 20 minutes depending on the type of greens. Add more water, 1 tablespoon at a time, as needed to prevent the greens from drying out.

3. Stir in the optional gomasio and salt. Serve hot.

NOTE: If using mature, bitter greens (such as mustard or dandelion greens), it's best to boil them for 10 minutes before adding them to the skillet.

This delicious side dish is particularly delightful with Indian menus. Let the onions cook for the full twenty minutes to caramelize them. This adds sweetness to the final dish.

indian spinach AND BROCCOLI PURÉE

MAKES 4 SERVINGS

1 tablespoon extra-virgin olive oil

1 tablespoon cold-pressed coconut oil

½ cup water

1½ cups thinly sliced onions

1 tablespoon peeled and grated fresh ginger

5 cups chopped broccoli

5 cups chopped spinach, lightly packed

1 teaspoon salt

1. Put the olive oil, coconut oil, ¼ cup of the water, and the onion and ginger in a large saucepan over medium-high heat. Cook, stirring frequently, for 5 minutes. Decrease the heat to medium-low, cover, and cook, stirring occasionally, until the onions are soft and lightly browned, about 20 minutes.

2. Stir in the broccoli, spinach, salt, and remaining ¼ cup of water. Decrease the heat to low, cover, and simmer until the vegetables are very tender, about 15 minutes. Let cool slightly.

3. Transfer the mixture to a food processor or blender and process until smooth, working in batches if need be. Serve hot.

These enticing, crispy, golden treats are a great way to introduce people to tofu, which is an excellent vegan source of protein, and tofu that is made with calcium chloride is also a good source of calcium (check the package label).

BAKED tofu fingers

1 pound firm or extra-firm tofu

¼ cup water

2 tablespoons reduced-sodium tamari

1 tablespoon cold-pressed sesame oil or extra-virgin olive oil

1. Preheat the oven to 350 degrees F.
2. Cut the tofu in half lengthwise, then slice each half ½ inch thick.
3. Put the water, tamari, and oil in a 13 x 9-inch baking pan and whisk until well blended. Arrange the tofu slices in the pan in a single layer, dipping each in the sauce and turning to coat it well on both sides.
4. Bake for 25 to 35 minutes, gently turning the slices over halfway through the cooking time; the longer the cooking time, the crispier the tofu.

This easy dish is a wonderful way to enjoy sweet potatoes. For a simple but thoroughly satisfying light meal, serve it in a bowl with Good Greens (page 154) spooned over the top, adding a handful of mung bean or lentil sprouts and finishing with a sprinkling of chopped fresh chives or green onions.

MASHED sweet potatoes

MAKES 3 SERVINGS

3 medium sweet potatoes, peeled and cut into large chunks (about 4 cups)

2 tablespoons cold-pressed coconut oil

1 tablespoon maple syrup or unrefined cane sugar

Pinch salt

1. Put 1 inch of water in a medium saucepan. Add the sweet potatoes and bring to a boil over high heat. Decrease the heat to medium-low, cover, and cook until tender, 20 to 25 minutes.
2. Drain well. Add the oil, maple syrup, and salt. Mash until smooth using a hand blender, potato masher, or large fork. Serve hot.

These superbly seasoned sweet potato chunks beautifully accent almost any meal. They're a particularly welcome addition to holiday meals and are featured in the menu on page 196.

baked sweet potatoes
WITH ROSEMARY AND MAPLE SYRUP

MAKES 6 SERVINGS

3 pounds sweet potatoes, scrubbed, halved crosswise, and cut into wedges (about 6 cups)

2 tablespoons extra-virgin olive oil

2 tablespoons maple syrup

2 tablespoons coarsely chopped fresh rosemary, or 1 tablespoon dried

Salt

1. Preheat the oven to 375 degrees F.
2. Put the sweet potatoes on a baking sheet or in a roasting pan. Drizzle with the oil and maple syrup and sprinkle with the rosemary. Mix with your hands until the sweet potatoes are evenly coated.
3. Bake uncovered for about 40 minutes, until tender and golden. Season with salt to taste. Serve hot.

For this versatile dish, use whatever vegetables you have on hand or use a larger proportion of vegetables that are in season. One caveat: It's best to use vegetables that require a similar baking time; otherwise, quick-cooking vegetables may get too soft before others get tender. The version here is perfect at the end of the summer. To turn this side dish into a substantial meal, serve it over cooked quinoa, millet, or brown rice.

BAKED mixed vegetables

MAKES 4 SERVINGS

½ cup water

2 tablespoons reduced-sodium tamari

1½ tablespoons extra-virgin olive oil

1 tablespoon minced garlic

1 teaspoon balsamic vinegar

1 teaspoon maple syrup

large pinch dried oregano

large pinch dried basil

1 small cauliflower, chopped

2 zucchini or yellow squash, halved lengthwise and sliced ¾ inch thick

2 red, orange, or yellow bell peppers, sliced

1½ cups sliced cremini or button mushrooms

1 cup sliced leek (see note, page 75) or chopped onion

1. Preheat the oven to 350 degrees F.

2. Put the water, tamari, oil, garlic, vinegar, maple syrup, oregano, and basil in a 3- or 4-quart casserole dish and whisk until well blended. Add the cauliflower, zucchini, bell peppers, mushrooms, and leek and stir until evenly coated.

3. Cover and bake for about 40 minutes, until all the vegetables are tender. Serve hot.

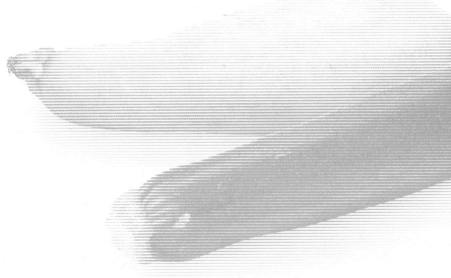

These fragrant and delectable mushrooms are a tasty accompaniment to any meal.

rosemary portobello MUSHROOMS

MAKES 4 SERVINGS

½ cup water

2 green onions, sliced

2 tablespoons reduced-sodium tamari

1 tablespoon extra-virgin olive oil

1 tablespoon freshly squeezed lemon juice

2 teaspoons chopped fresh rosemary, or 1 teaspoon dried, crushed

1 small clove garlic, minced

3 portobello mushrooms, halved crosswise and sliced ½ inch thick (4 to 5 cups)

1. Preheat the oven to 325 degrees F.

2. Put the water, green onions, tamari, oil, lemon juice, rosemary, and garlic in a 13 x 9-inch baking pan and whisk until well blended. Add the mushrooms and stir gently until evenly coated.

3. Bake uncovered for about 40 minutes, until tender and lightly browned, stirring occasionally to coat the mushrooms with the sauce. Serve hot.

These colorful fries are delicious on their own but are also tasty dipped in ketchup. They're a great way to win people over to a variety of root vegetables. Try using a combination of three or more vegetables. Choosing types with different colors makes for an attractive presentation, and also for more well-rounded nutrition.

ROOT fries

8 cups root vegetables (such as potatoes, sweet potatoes, beets, carrots, turnips, parships, rutabagas), **scrubbed and cut into French-fry shapes**

1 onion or leek (see note, page 75), **sliced**

8 cloves garlic, peeled

3 tablespoons extra-virgin olive oil

1 teaspoon dried rosemary or thyme, crushed

Salt

1. Preheat the oven to 375 degrees F.
2. Put the root vegetables, onion, and garlic in two large, shallow baking pans. Sprinkle with the oil and rosemary and toss until evenly coated.
3. Bake uncovered for 35 to 45 minutes, until all the vegetables are tender and lightly browned, turning them with a spatula occasionally during cooking. Season with salt to taste. Serve hot.

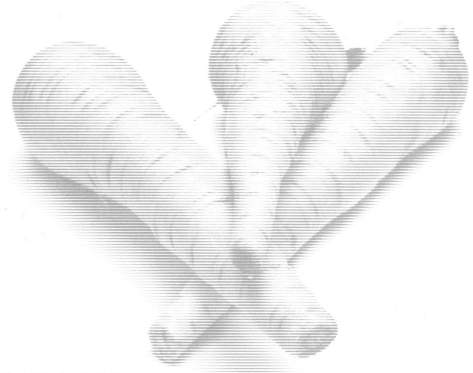

The deeply flavorful marinade in this dish concentrates as it cooks, coating and infusing the tender chunks of potato. For a wonderful meal, serve it with Millet-Rice Patties (page 132), steamed seasonal vegetables, and a crisp green salad.

roasted new potatoes WITH TARRAGON VINAIGRETTE

MAKES 4 SERVINGS

1 cup water

¼ cup extra-virgin olive oil

2 tablespoons reduced-sodium tamari

2 tablespoons cider vinegar

1 tablespoon minced garlic

2 teaspoons dried tarragon, crushed

2 pounds small new red or white potatoes, scrubbed and quartered (about 4 cups)

½ cup finely chopped onion

1. Preheat the oven to 350 degrees F.

2. Put the water, oil, tamari, vinegar, garlic, and tarragon in a 13 x 9-inch baking pan and whisk until well blended. Add the potatoes and onion and stir until evenly coated.

3. Bake uncovered for about 1½ hours, stirring every 20 minutes, until the liquid has mostly evaporated and the potatoes are golden and fork-tender. For optimum flavor, serve at room temperature.

This is a creamy and delicious dairy-free version of a classic fall and winter dish.

SCALLOPED potatoes

MAKES 6 TO 8 SERVINGS

1 cup raw cashews, soaked in water for 4 hours (see note, page 68)

4 cups water

1 onion, finely chopped

2 tablespoons chopped celery

1½ tablespoons arrowroot powder

1 tablespoon nutritional yeast

1 teaspoon salt

8 medium gold or russet potatoes, peeled and thinly sliced

1. Preheat the oven to 350 degrees F.

2. Drain and rinse the cashews. Transfer to a blender.

3. Add 2 cups of the water, and process until completely smooth.

4. Add the remaining 2 cups of water, 1 tablespoon of the onion, and the celery, arrowroot powder, nutritional yeast, and salt and process until smooth.

5. Pour the mixture into a medium saucepan. Bring to a boil over medium-high heat, stirring constantly. Decrease the heat to medium and cook, stirring frequently, until thick, about 5 minutes.

6. Spread a thin layer of the cashew mixture in a 4-quart casserole dish. Top with a layer of one-third of the potatoes and onions, then pour one-third of the remaining cashew mixture evenly over the top. Repeat twice more, for a total of three layers.

7. Cover and bake for 1½ hours, until bubbly and browned and the potatoes are fork-tender, removing the cover halfway through the baking time. Serve hot.

Here's is a fancy and flavorful way to enjoy brown rice as a side dish.

rice pilaf WITH NUTS AND RAISINS

2 tablespoons extra-virgin olive oil

¼ cup water

1½ cups finely chopped onions

1 tablespoon minced garlic

1 teaspoon peeled and grated fresh ginger

2 cups brown jasmine rice, soaked in water for 4 to 8 hours (see note)

3 cups boiling water

1 tablespoon cold-pressed coconut oil

1 cup chopped pecans

1 cup raisins

½ teaspoon salt

½ teaspoon grated lemon zest

½ teaspoon grated orange zest

1. Put the olive oil, water, onions, garlic, and ginger in a medium saucepan over medium heat. Cook, stirring frequently, for 8 minutes.

2. Drain and rinse the rice. Add the rice to the onion mixture and cook, stirring occasionally, for 5 minutes.

3. Pour in the boiling water. Decrease the heat to medium-low, cover, and cook undisturbed for 40 minutes, until the water is absorbed and the rice is tender. Let stand, covered, for 5 minutes.

4. Melt the coconut oil in a heavy skillet over medium-low heat. Add the pecans and cook, stirring frequently, until lightly browned, about 5 minutes. Stir in the raisins, salt, lemon zest, and orange zest. Cook and stir for 1 minute.

5. Add the pecan mixture to the rice and stir gently until well combined. Serve hot.

NOTE: If you don't have time to soak the rice, increase the amount of boiling water to 3½ cups.

Variation: There are many varieties of brown rice and any of them could be used for this recipe. Either brown basmati rice or short-grain brown rice would be a good choice. You could also use a rice blend or replace part of the brown rice with black, red, or wild rice.

Dahl can be eaten as a side dish, spooned over rice or vegetables, or used as a dip for bread. Leftovers can be thinned with water or vegetable broth for a tasty soup. This dahl is fabulous served over brown jasmine rice, with side dishes of Potato-Cauliflower Curry (page 147) and Indian Spinach and Broccoli Purée (page 155) for an Indian-style meal.

CLASSIC dahl

2 cups yellow split peas, brown or red lentils, or mung beans, soaked in water for 8 hours

4 cups water, plus more as needed

3 tablespoons cold-pressed coconut oil

2½ tablespoons ground coriander

1½ tablespoons ground cumin

2¼ teaspoons ground turmeric

1 large onion, halved and sliced

1½ teaspoons salt

1. Drain and rinse the split peas. Transfer to a medium pot. Add the water. If it doesn't cover the split peas by 2 inches, add more water as needed. Bring to a boil over high heat. Decrease the heat to medium-low, cover, and simmer, stirring occasionally, until the peas are tender and falling apart, between 15 and 60 minutes depending on the type and age of legumes used (see note). Add water as needed to maintain a thick but soupy consistency.

2. Heat the oil in a heavy skillet over medium heat. Add the coriander, cumin, and turmeric and cook, stirring constantly, until fragrant, about 1 minute, taking care not to burn the spices.

3. Stir in the onion. Decrease the heat to medium-low, cover, and simmer, stirring occasionally, until soft, about 15 minutes, adding a bit of water as needed to prevent sticking.

4. Stir the onion mixture and salt into to the cooked peas. Cook over medium-low heat, stirring frequently, for 10 to 15 minutes, adding water as needed to keep the mixture thick but soupy. Serve hot.

NOTE: Red lentils will cook in about 15 minutes, whereas brown lentils or mung beans could take up to 40 minutes, and split peas could take 60 minutes or longer.

Tempeh, made from fermented ground soybeans, is one of the best ways to enjoy these protein-packed legumes, since they become more digestible through the fermentation process. Look for tempeh in the refrigerator or freezer section of natural food stores or well-stocked grocery stores. This simple side dish adds a grounding quality to vegetable-based meals.

sweet-and-savory BAKED TEMPEH

MAKES 3 TO 4 SERVINGS

½ cup freshly squeezed orange juice (about 1 orange) or unsweetened apple juice

1½ tablespoons cold-pressed sesame oil

1 tablespoon reduced-sodium tamari

1 tablespoon maple syrup

8 ounces tempeh, sliced ½ inch thick

⅓ cup thinly sliced red onion or leek (see note, page 75)

1. Preheat the oven to 350 degrees F.
2. Put the orange juice, oil, tamari, and maple syrup in a 13 x 9-inch baking pan and whisk until well blended. Add the tempeh and onion and stir gently until evenly coated.
3. Cover and bake for 20 minutes. Uncover and bake for 15 minutes. Serve hot.

The secret is in the sauce! In this recipe, classic Mexican ingredients and seasonings come together to create a tantalizing tempeh dish.

cilantro TEMPEH

MAKES 4 SERVINGS

2 tablespoons cold-pressed sesame oil

¾ cup water, plus more as needed

1 cup sliced onion

2 teaspoons minced garlic

½ teaspoon ground coriander

½ teaspoon ground cumin

¼ teaspoon cayenne

8 ounces tempeh, diced

3 tablespoons cider vinegar

1 cup chopped tomato

½ red bell pepper, chopped

½ cup chopped fresh cilantro

½ teaspoon salt

1. Put the oil, ¼ cup of the water, and the onion in a medium skillet over medium-high heat. Cook and stir for 5 minutes.

2. Decrease the heat to medium. Stir in the garlic, coriander, cumin, and cayenne and cook, stirring frequently for 3 minutes. Add more water as needed to prevent sticking.

3. Stir in the tempeh, the remaining ½ cup of water, and the vinegar. Decrease the heat to medium-low, cover, and cook, stirring occasionally, for 15 minutes.

4. Uncover, increase the heat to medium, and cook, stirring occasionally, until the liquid is reduced by about half, about 8 minutes.

5. Stir in the tomato, pepper, cilantro, and salt. Cook briefly, just until steaming hot. Serve immediately.

CHAPTER 12

Desserts and Sweets

This treat satisfies cravings for both popcorn and something sweet. It is, of course, the perfect thing to munch on while watching a movie.

sweet spiced POPCORN

4 cups air-popped popcorn (about ½ cup popcorn kernels)

2 tablespoons cold-pressed coconut oil

2 tablespoons maple syrup

1 tablespoon light molasses

1 teaspoon vanilla extract

1 teaspoon ground cinnamon

Pinch salt

1. Put the popcorn in a large bowl.

2. Put the oil, maple syrup, molasses, and vanilla extract in a small saucepan over low heat. Stir until warm and well blended, about 2 minutes. Remove from the heat and stir in the cinnamon and salt.

3. Pour the warm mixture over the popcorn, stirring gently to coat the kernels evenly. Serve immediately.

Keep these easy-to-make, wholesome treats in the freezer and pull one or two out when you're looking for a little something that is rich and sweet.

VANILLA bliss balls

MAKES 18 BALLS

2 cups walnuts

2 tablespoons maple syrup

1 teaspoon vanilla extract

Pinch salt

½ cup raw cashews

½ cup raisins

1. Put the walnuts in a food processor and process until creamy and almost smooth.

2. Add the maple syrup, vanilla extract, and salt and process until well combined.

3. Add the cashews and raisins and process until evenly distributed but not completely smooth; the mixture should retain some texture.

4. Roll into 1-inch balls and place them in a single layer in a sealable container.

5. Cover and freeze for at least 1 hour. Vanilla Bliss Balls can be eaten frozen or after thawing for up to 15 minutes.

6. Stored in a sealed container in the freezer, Vanilla Bliss Balls will keep for 3 months.

If you're health-minded yet still want a little something rich, sweet, and chocolaty, these raw truffles are the perfect fix.

CHOCOLATE truffles

MAKES 18 TRUFFLES

¾ cup walnuts

¾ cup raw cashews

¾ cup pitted soft dates

2 tablespoons unsweetened cocoa powder, plus more as needed

1 to 3 tablespoons water, as needed

1. Put the walnuts and cashews in a food processor and process until finely ground.

2. Add the dates and process until smooth.

3. Add the cocoa powder and process until well combined. Test to see if the mixture holds together by squeezing a tablespoonful of it in your hand. If it doesn't hold together, add water, 1 tablespoon at a time, processing after each addition, until the mixture holds together.

4. Roll into 1-inch balls and place them in a single layer in a sealable container.

5. Cover and refrigerate for at least 1 hour.

6. Stored in a sealed container in the freezer, Chocolate Truffles will keep for 3 months. They can be eaten frozen or after thawing for up to 15 minutes.

The spices in this raw pudding combine to create a deeply nourishing treat that's nutritious enough to eat for breakfast. Chia seeds, an ancient food dating back to the Aztecs, contain impressive amounts of omega-3 fatty acids, protein, minerals, and fiber. They give this pudding a texture similar to fine tapioca.

spiced chia PUDDING

MAKES 6 SERVINGS

1 cup raw almonds, soaked in water for 4 hours

4 cups water

8 pitted soft dates

1 teaspoon ground cinnamon

½ teaspoon ground allspice

½ teaspoon ground cloves

¼ teaspoon ground nutmeg

¾ cup raisins

¾ cup white or black chia seeds

Maple syrup or unrefined cane sugar, for garnish

1. Drain and rinse the almonds. Transfer to a blender.

2. Add the water, dates, cinnamon, allspice, cloves, and nutmeg and process until the almonds are very finely ground.

3. Strain into a medium bowl through a nut milk bag, fine-mesh strainer, or regular strainer lined with cheesecloth. Press or squeeze the solids to extract as much liquid as possible. Discard the solids.

4. Add the raisins and chia seeds to the liquid. Let sit at room temperature for 2 to 3 hours, stirring about every 30 minutes. The chia seeds and raisins will absorb the liquid and create a thick pudding.

5. Serve at room temperature or chilled, garnished with a drizzle of maple syrup or a sprinkling of sugar.

6. Stored in a sealed container in the refrigerator, Spiced Chia Pudding will keep for 4 days.

People will never guess that the secret to this amazing, creamy raw pie is avocados.

CHOCOLATE mousse pie

See photo facing page 147.

MAKES 6 TO 8 SERVINGS

1 cup raw almonds

20 pitted soft dates (see note)

¼ cup maple syrup, plus more as needed (see note)

3 ripe avocados (enough to yield about 4 cups of mashed avocado)

3 tablespoons unsweetened cocoa powder, plus more as needed (see note)

1 cup mashed fresh or thawed frozen berries

1. To make the crust, put the almonds in a food processor and process until finely ground.

2. Add 3 of the dates and process until the texture is uniform. If needed, add maple syrup, 1 teaspoon at a time, until the mixture sticks together. Press the mixture into the bottom and sides of an 8-inch pie pan.

3. To make the filling, put the avocado flesh in a food processor. Add the 17 remaining dates and the maple syrup and cocoa powder and process until completely smooth. Taste and add more cocoa powder or maple syrup if desired.

4. Pour the filling into the crust and refrigerate for at least 2 hours. Serve chilled, topping with the berries just before serving or passing the berries at the table.

5. Covered tightly and stored in the refrigerator, Chocolate Mousse Pie will keep for 3 days.

NOTE: Because avocados vary in size and dates vary both in size and sweetness, you may need to add extra cocoa powder and maple syrup. Add enough cocoa powder so there's no hint of green, and add more maple syrup if necessary to achieve the desired sweetness.

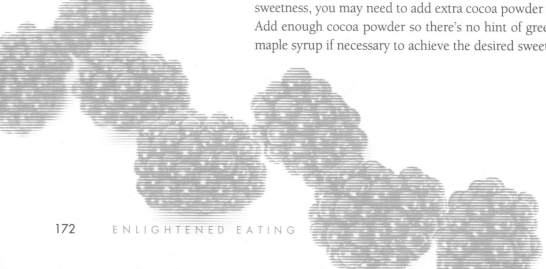

This is the perfect fall dessert, made with loads of fruit and minimal added sugar. For extra indulgence, serve it topped with Cashew Cream (page 180).

apple CRISP

MAKES 4 SERVINGS

4 cups peeled and sliced apples

¾ cup unsweetened apple juice

½ cup plus 1 tablespoon spelt flour or whole wheat flour

1 teaspoon ground cinnamon

¼ cup unrefined cane sugar

¼ cup expeller-pressed sunflower oil

¼ teaspoon salt

½ cup old-fashioned rolled oats

Cashew Cream (page 180), for garnish

1. Preheat the oven to 350 degrees F.

2. Put the apples in an 8-inch square baking pan. Pour in ½ cup of the apple juice. Sprinkle 1 tablespoon of the flour and the cinnamon over the apples. Stir gently until well combined.

3. Put the remaining ¼ cup of apple juice and the sugar, oil, and salt in a medium bowl and whisk until well blended.

4. Add the oats and remaining ½ cup of flour and stir to combine. Sprinkle the mixture evenly over the apples.

5. Bake for 45 minutes, until golden brown. Serve warm, topped with Cashew Cream if desired.

6. Stored in a sealed container in the refrigerator, Apple Crisp will keep for 5 days.

Ten minutes is all the time you'll need to put together these sweet and crispy snack bars. No baking required!

fruit, nut, and cereal BARS

MAKES 16 BARS

¾ cup raw almond butter

¼ cup brown rice syrup

¼ cup maple syrup

1 tablespoon cold-pressed coconut oil

3 cups corn flakes

½ cup raisins

½ cup chopped raw almonds

1. Oil an 8-inch square baking pan.

2. Put the almond butter, brown rice syrup, maple syrup, and oil in a medium saucepan over medium-low heat. Stir frequently until warm and well combined, about 5 minutes.

3. Remove from the heat. Gently stir in the corn flakes, raisins, and almonds. Transfer to the prepared pan and gently pat into an even layer.

4. Refrigerate for at least 1 hour to set up before cutting into 2-inch squares.

5. Stored in a sealed container at room temperature, Fruit, Nut, and Cereal Bars will keep for 10 days.

Variations

- Replace the almond butter with cashew or peanut butter.
- Replace the corn flakes with rice flakes or millet flakes cereal.
- Replace the raisins with dried cranberries or chopped dried apricots.
- Replace the almonds with pumpkin seeds.

Enjoy this zesty version of classic date squares.

LEMON-DATE squares

MAKES 16 SQUARES

2 cups pitted soft dates, chopped

⅓ cup water

¼ cup freshly squeezed lemon juice
(about 1 large lemon)

¾ cup unrefined cane sugar

½ cup expeller-pressed sunflower oil

1¾ cups spelt flour or whole wheat
flour

1 teaspoon salt

½ teaspoon baking soda

1 cup old-fashioned rolled oats

1. Preheat the oven to 350 degrees F.

2. Oil an 8-inch square baking pan.

3. Put the dates, water, and lemon juice in a medium saucepan over medium-low heat. Cover and cook, stirring occasionally, until the dates start falling apart, about 15 minutes.

4. Put the sugar and oil in a medium bowl and stir vigorously until well combined. Stir in the flour, salt, and baking soda. Add the oats and mix well with your hands. The mixture should be crumbly but hold together when squeezed.

5. Press two-thirds of the flour mixture into the prepared baking pan in an even layer. Spread the date mixture evenly over the top. Crumble the remaining flour mixture evenly over the top. Lightly pack the top layer with your hands.

6. Bake for 30 minutes, until golden brown. Let cool completely in the pan before cutting into 2-inch squares.

7. Stored in a sealed container in the refrigerator, Lemon-Date Squares will keep for 1 week.

These blondies are rich tasting and chewy. The combination of rice syrup and maple syrup mimics the flavor of butterscotch extremely well.

butterscotch blondies
WITH CHOCOLATE CHIPS AND DRIED CHERRIES

MAKES 16 BLONDIES

1 cup spelt flour or whole wheat flour

¾ cup barley flour

1 teaspoon baking powder

½ teaspoon baking soda

¼ teaspoon salt

⅓ cup brown rice syrup

⅓ cup maple syrup

⅓ cup expeller-pressed sunflower oil

1 tablespoon vanilla extract

½ cup vegan chocolate chips

⅓ cup dried tart cherries or dried cranberries

1. Preheat the oven to 350 degrees F.

2. Line an 8-inch square baking pan with parchment paper, or oil and flour the pan.

3. Put the spelt flour, barley flour, baking powder, baking soda, and salt in a medium bowl and mix well.

4. Put the brown rice syrup, maple syrup, oil, and vanilla extract in a large bowl and whisk until well blended. Stir in the chocolate chips and cherries.

5. Add the flour mixture and stir to combine. The batter will be fairly thick and sticky.

6. Pour into the prepared pan and smooth the top with a rubber spatula.

7. Bake for 20 to 25 minutes, until a toothpick inserted in the center comes out fairly clean. Don't overbake, or the blondies will be dry. The blondies will deflate a little as they cool.

8. Let cool completely in the pan before cutting into 2-inch squares.

9. Stored in a sealed container at room temperature, Butterscotch Blondies will keep for 1 week.

Contributed by permission of Ricki Heller, dietdessertndogs.com.

These flourless, calcium-rich cookies are rich, chewy, and wonderful.

COCONUT macaroons

¾ cup raw almonds

2 tablespoons finely ground flaxseeds

⅛ teaspoon salt

2 cups unsweetened shredded dried coconut

½ cup maple syrup

¼ cup tahini

1 teaspoon vanilla extract

1. Preheat the oven to 350 degrees F.
2. Lightly oil two baking sheets.
3. Put the almonds, flaxseeds, and salt in a food processor and process until very finely ground. Add the coconut and pulse a few times to combine.
4. Add the maple syrup, tahini, and vanilla extract. Process just until well blended and the mixture forms a sticky ball, stopping occasionally to scrape down the work bowl with a rubber spatula if needed. Stop processing as soon as the mixture holds together to avoid grinding the coconut too finely.
5. Drop rounded tablespoons of the dough onto the prepared baking sheets, spacing them about 1 inch apart. Wet your palms and flatten the dough slightly.
6. Bake for 10 to 12 minutes, until golden brown on top, rotating the baking sheets after about 5 minutes.
7. Let cool completely on the baking sheets. The macaroons will firm up as they cool.
8. Stored in a sealed container at room temperature, Coconut Macaroons will keep for 1 week.

Contributed by permission of Ricki Heller, dietdessertndogs.com.

This is a wholesome, sweet, and chewy alternative to traditional chocolate chip cookies.

oatmeal–chocolate chip COOKIES

MAKES ABOUT 24 COOKIES

1 cup old-fashioned rolled oats

1 cup spelt flour or whole wheat flour

¼ cup hempseeds

½ teaspoon baking soda

½ teaspoon salt

⅓ cup almond butter or peanut butter

2 tablespoons cold-pressed coconut oil, melted

1 cup unrefined cane sugar

½ cup Homemade Almond Milk (page 52) or other nondairy milk

2 teaspoons vanilla extract

⅔ cup vegan chocolate chips

⅓ cup coarsely chopped walnuts or pecans

1. Preheat the oven to 325 degrees F.

2. Lightly oil two large baking sheets.

3. Put the oats, flour, hempseeds, baking soda, and salt in a large bowl and mix well.

4. Put the almond butter and oil in a medium bowl and stir vigorously until well blended. Add the sugar, almond milk, and vanilla extract and stir until well combined.

5. Add the sugar mixture to the flour mixture. Stir to combine, using as few strokes as possible. Gently stir in the chocolate chips and walnuts.

6. Drop the dough onto the prepared baking sheets, using 2 rounded tablespoons of dough per cookie and spacing them about 2 inches apart.

7. Bake for 13 to 15 minutes, until the tops are set and look dry.

8. Let cool on the baking sheets for 5 minutes before transferring to wire racks to cool completely.

9. Stored in a sealed container at room temperature, Oatmeal–Chocolate Chip Cookies will keep for 10 days.

This is a fast and delicious chocolate treat. Mix it right in the pan, bake, and drizzle with a simple chocolate glaze. For a special presentation, serve it topped with Cashew Cream (page 180) or with fresh fruit on the side.

SIX-MINUTE chocolate cake

MAKES 8 SERVINGS

1½ cups spelt flour or whole wheat flour

1 cup unrefined cane sugar

⅔ cup unsweetened cocoa powder

1 teaspoon baking soda

½ teaspoon plus 1 pinch salt

1 cup cold water

½ cup expeller-pressed sunflower oil

2 teaspoons vanilla extract

2 tablespoons cider vinegar

2 tablespoons cold-pressed coconut oil, melted

⅓ cup maple syrup

1. Preheat the oven to 375 degrees F.
2. Put the flour, sugar, ⅓ cup of the cocoa powder, the baking soda, and ½ teaspoon of the salt in an 8-inch square baking pan or a 9-inch round baking pan and stir to combine.
3. Combine the water, sunflower oil, and vanilla extract in a 2-cup measuring cup and whisk until well blended.
4. Pour the oil mixture into the flour mixture in the baking pan and stir with a fork or small whisk until smooth.
5. Add the vinegar and stir quickly. There will be pale swirls in the batter where the baking soda and the vinegar are reacting. Stir just until the vinegar is evenly distributed throughout the batter.
6. Bake for 25 to 30 minutes, until a toothpick inserted in the center comes out clean.
7. Let cool completely in the pan.
8. To make a glaze, melt the coconut oil in a small saucepan. Add the maple syrup, the remaining ⅓ cup cocoa powder, and the pinch of salt. Mix with a hand blender or a whisk until smooth.
9. Drizzle the glaze over the cooled cake. Refrigerate uncovered for at least 30 minutes before serving. Serve chilled or at room temperature.
10. Covered tightly and stored in the refrigerator, Six-Minute Chocolate Cake will keep for 1 week.

This is a delicious and easy alternative to whipped cream. Serve it as a topping for fruit crumbles and crisps, pies, cakes, or other baked goods, or spoon it over sliced fresh fruit or berries.

cashew CREAM

MAKES 1½ CUPS

1 cup raw cashews, soaked in water for 4 hours (see note, page 68)

1½ cups water

3 pitted soft dates, or 2 tablespoons maple syrup

Pinch salt

1. Drain and rinse the cashews. Transfer to a blender.
2. Add the water, dates, and salt and process until completely smooth and creamy.
3. Transfer to a glass jar and refrigerate until ready to serve. Stored in a sealed jar in the refrigerator, Cashew Cream will keep for 4 days.

APPENDIX A

Cooking Beans and Grains

Whole grains and legumes provide the backbone of a healthful whole-foods diet, yet many people are unfamiliar with cooking them from scratch. If that sounds like you, here are general instructions for cooking each.

Cooking Beans

1. Measure out the amount of dried beans needed. For every cup of cooked beans, use about ⅓ cup of dried beans. Smaller beans and lentils may need about ½ cup dried to equal 1 cup cooked.

2. Pick through the dried beans, discarding stones and any blemished beans.

3. Rinse the beans in a colander.

4. For best digestion and even cooking, soak the beans before cooking. Put them in a pot or bowl and add water to cover by about 3 inches. Soak for 8 hours at room temperature or for up to 3 days in the refrigerator.

5. Drain in a colander and rinse thoroughly.

6. Put the beans in a pot and cover with fresh water by 2 inches.

7. Bring to a boil over high heat for 5 minutes, then drain the cooking liquid along with any foam that may have formed. Rinse the beans.

8. Rinse the pot and return the beans to it. Add fresh water to cover by 2 inches.

9. Add a 4-inch strip of kombu for every cup of dried beans if desired. Kombu is a sea vegetable that improves the digestibility of beans. It also adds beneficial minerals to the bean broth.

10. Don't add salt prior to cooking, as it will toughen the skins of the beans.

Beans, Beans . . .

In terms of a plant-based diet, many people find they have a hard time digesting legumes, especially if they aren't accustomed to eating them. You can improve the digestibility of legumes by soaking them for four to eight hours, then draining and rinsing them well. When cooking them, adding a piece of kombu (a type of sea vegetable) can enhance digestibility. Another option is adding vinegar to the final dish. Many of the spices used to season legumes in traditional cultures can also help, such as turmeric and ginger, which are used in Indian cuisine.

11. Bring to a boil over medium-high heat. Decrease the heat to medium-low, cover, and simmer, until the beans are tender. Cooking time depends on the size and age of the beans but usually ranges from 45 to 90 minutes. However, larger or older beans could take much longer—up to 3 hours. The finished beans should be tender and easy to mash against the roof of your mouth with your tongue.

12. For convenience and economy, cook large quantities of beans and freeze the extras in 2-cup portions.

Note: Don't mix beans from two different purchases when cooking. They can take significantly different amounts of times to cook, so you could end up with some beans that are too soft and others that are undercooked. If only a small amount of beans remains after measuring out the dried amount, go ahead and add them in so you won't be inclined to mix batches the next time you cook with that type of bean.

Cooking Grains

1. Measure out the amount of dry grains needed. For every 2½ cups of cooked grains, use about 1 cup of dry grains. (Certain grains will yield slightly more than 2½ cups.)

2. For best digestion and even cooking, grains should ideally be soaked in water for 4 to 8 hours prior to cooking.

3. Drain in a colander or, for small grains like quinoa, a fine-mesh strainer, then rinse thoroughly.

4. Transfer to a saucepan and add water. For each cup of dry grains prior to soaking, use 1½ cups of water. If you didn't soak the grains, use 2 cups of water for each cup of dry grains.

5. Bring to a boil over high heat. Decrease the heat to medium low, cover, and simmer for the amount of time indicated below:
   - Barley (hulled): 35 to 40 minutes
   - Brown rice: 35 to 40 minutes
   - Buckwheat groats: 15 minutes
   - Millet: 40 to 45 minutes
   - Quinoa: 15 to 20 minutes
   - Wild rice: 40 minutes

6. Turn off the heat and let stand, covered, for 5 minutes. Fluff with a fork.

Note: Recipes for loaves or patties that include instructions for cooking grains might call for a bit more water than specified here to create a stickier consistency.

Glossary of Select Ingredients

Because the recipes in this cookbook focus on fresh, in-season produce, most of the ingredients will be familiar and readily available. However, a few ingredients I call for may seem unusual, so they are described here. Look for these ingredients at your local natural food store or in the natural foods section of your grocery store.

Arrowroot powder. Arrowroot powder, a starch from the tubers of the arrowroot plant, is used for thickening. It's preferable to cornstarch because it's less processed.

Balsamic vinegar. A reddish brown Italian vinegar made from grapes and aged in wooden barrels, balsamic vinegar has a rich sweet-and-sour taste.

Chia seeds. An ancient food dating back to the Aztecs, chia seeds are considered a superfood because they contain high amounts of essential fatty acids, protein, minerals, and fiber.

Chili sauce. Rather than using whole chile peppers to add heat to dishes, you may find it more convenient to have a bottle of prepared chili sauce on hand. Look for chili sauces at ethnic markets or with Asian foods in grocery stores or natural food markets.

Cider vinegar, raw. Also known as apple cider vinegar, the cider vinegar I recommend is a raw, unprocessed vinegar made from fermented apple juice.

Coconut oil, cold-pressed. Cold-pressed coconut oil is unrefined oil extracted from fresh coconuts. Don't confuse it with coconut butter, which is blended whole coconut flesh and therefore contains the meat of the coconut in addition to the oil.

Dates, soft. Avoid the dried, compressed dates available at many supermarkets. Soft dates, such as medjools, can be purchased in the produce section at some grocery stores or from Middle Eastern markets or natural food stores. They are usually sold refrigerated, and you should keep them in the refrigerator at home. They are a nutritious food, and in addition to being delicious eaten on their own, they can be used as an alternative sweetener, particularly in blended mixtures.

Dulse. Dulse is a sea vegetable that can be purchased dried in flake or leaf form. Like all sea vegetables, it is high in trace minerals.

Ginger. Fresh ginger can be found in the produce section of grocery stores. It keeps best at room temperature. (When it's kept in the refrigerator, it tends to get moldy.) Simply cut off the amount needed, remove the dry end from the previous cut, and peel.

Gluten-free grains. Gluten is a protein contained in many grains, including barley, Kamut, rye, spelt, and wheat. It is one of the most common allergens and can also be hard to digest for some people. The most common gluten-free grains are buckwheat, millet, quinoa, and rice.

Hempseeds. High in protein, minerals, and essential fatty acids, hempseeds can be added to smoothies or sprinkled on salads or fruit bowls. Note that hempseed oil has a distinctive taste that may take some getting used to. You may wish to start with just a small proportion of hempseed oil and increase it as your taste buds adapt.

Kombu. Kombu is a sea vegetable that is often added when cooking beans to help make them more digestible.

Miso. A salty, fermented paste that originated in Japan, miso is typically made from soybeans but may also contain other beans, grains, or a combination of beans and grains. Being fermented, it's rich in active enzymes and probiotics, or friendly bacteria. It's often used as a base for soups but is best added after the soup is removed from the heat, as boiling destroys its enzymes and probiotics. Look for unpasteurized miso in the refrigerated section at health food stores or Asian markets.

Molasses. Molasses is the syrupy by-product of the process of refining sugarcane into table sugar. Blackstrap molasses is made from the third boiling of the sugar syrup and is therefore the most concentrated liquid that remains after the sugar's sucrose has been crystallized. Blackstrap molasses is very dark and thick and has an intense, deep flavor. It is less sweet than other types of molasses, but it is rich in minerals, especially calcium, copper, manganese, potassium, and magnesium.

Nondairy milk. Alternative milks are made from a variety of plant foods, including almonds, coconut, hempseeds, rice, and soybeans. It's convenient to purchase it ready-made, but you can also make it yourself (see pages 52 to 53).

Nutritional yeast. Nutritional yeast is a tasty form of deactivated yeast that adds a cheesy flavor to recipes. It also contains a wide range of B vitamins.

Salt. Salt can come from a variety of sources. Common table salt is refined and contains only sodium and chloride, plus anticaking chemicals and, usually, iodine, whereas sea salt contains the wide array of trace minerals naturally present in the sea. Many chefs prefer the depth of flavor of sea salt, and seemingly endless varieties are now available to experiment with.

Sesame oil. As noted in the recipes, I recommend cold-pressed sesame oil. Because toasting sesame seeds can damage the nutritious fats they contain, I also recommend not using toasted sesame oil.

Spelt flour. Spelt is an ancient grain similar to wheat but higher in nutrients and lower in gluten. Spelt flour can be substituted for wheat flour on a one-to-one basis. When making baked goods, you might want to use light spelt flour, which has some of the bran removed to help create a lighter final product.

Tahini. Tahini is a thick, smooth paste is made by grinding raw or toasted sesame seeds.

Tamari. Tamari is naturally brewed soy sauce that contains no sugar or preservatives. It has a deeper flavor than conventional soy sauces. Because tamari is high in sodium, look for reduced-sodium varieties, which are just as flavorful.

Tempeh. Tempeh is a healthful fermented soybean product often found in the freezer section at natural food stores. It can be sliced or cubed and used to add protein to recipes.

Tofu. High in protein and highly versatile, tofu comes in two main varieties: silken tofu, a Japanese style with a smoother consistency, which can be used in sauces, puddings, dressings, and baked goods; and regular, a Chinese style that's usually firmer and denser and lends itself well to stir-fries, nondairy alternatives to cottage cheese and feta cheese, and sandwich spreads. Look for organic brands, as most nonorganic soybeans are genetically modified. A new innovation is tofu made from sprouted soybeans, which is a good choice because sprouting makes soybeans more digestible and increases the availability of their nutrients.

Unrefined cane sugar. Unrefined cane sugar is a brown, powdery, minimally refined sweetener that is essentially dried and granulated sugarcane juice. Therefore, it contains most of the nutrients present in sugarcane juice. It can be used interchangeably with refined sugar.

APPENDIX C
Recommended Kitchen Equipment

I f you spend much time in the kitchen working with food, it's helpful, pleasant, and efficient to have good-quality equipment. That being said, the cost can add up, so use what you have and upgrade as you're able or as old kitchen tools and equipment wear out. Alternatively, you can look for used kitchen equipment at online sites or perhaps purchase items from friends or family members who aren't using them anymore.

Blender. A blender is essential for smoothies, sauces, and some blended soups. Most home blenders will do, but you may eventually want to purchase a powerful high-speed blender, such as a Vitamix or a Total Blender by Blendtec.

Cutting boards. Along with a chef's knife, good cutting boards are essential to a whole-foods kitchen. Wood is the best surface to cut on. Rub your cutting boards with coconut oil to minimize stains, odor retention, and contamination. Surprisingly, wooden boards are less prone to bacterial growth than plastic cutting boards. Another nice feature is that their surfaces have some give, absorbing the impact of the knife blade and making it easier to cut through food. Have at least two cutting boards so you can keep one separate for fruit, nuts, and any other ingredients that you don't want to pick up the flavor and aroma of garlic and onions from your main cutting board.

Food processor. Food processors are ideal for fine chopping, grating large quantities of ingredients, and puréeing mixtures for desserts and spreads. A machine with a 7- to 12-cup bowl works well for most recipes. Cuisinart brand is recommended by most chefs, and I agree.

Hand blender. Also known as an immersion blender, this versatile device is handy for use with larger volumes or smaller amounts, if you use the blending cup included with it. With a hand blender, you can purée an entire pot of soup at once, avoiding the need to transfer the soup to a stand blender or work in batches. A hand blender also makes for speedier cleanup. Some models come with a whisk attachment, which you may find useful.

Juicer. A juicer is a wonderful addition to any health-conscious cook's kitchen. Green Star and Omega Vertical are good-quality choices. I recommend either a twin-gear juicer or a masticating juicer (single gear or upright), which operates at slower speeds. Both types are powerful and easy to clean and typically come with an extended warranty. Both work well on vegetables, fruits, and wheatgrass, extracting a maximum amount of juice while maintaining low temperatures and high nutrient content.

Knives. A good-quality 8-inch chef's knife is one of the most important tools in a whole-foods kitchen. Buy the best knives you can afford, preferably high-carbon steel, and keep them sharp. Most home cooks only need an 8-inch chef's knife, a paring knife, and a small serrated knife.

Nut milk bags. Durable nylon bags made specifically for straining homemade nut-based milks are readily available online, or you might find them at your local natural food store. They make preparing nondairy milk at home a breeze.

Personal blender or coffee grinder. A personal blender or coffee grinder comes in handy when grinding small batches of nuts, seeds, or spices. If you opt for a personal blender, you can also take it with you when traveling to make smoothies.

Stocking Your Kitchen and Storage Tips

If you're new to cooking with whole foods or haven't used many fresh vegetables and fruits in the past, you may wonder about storage. Here are some pointers on foods to keep on hand, how to store them, and for how long.

Fruits

Fresh fruits in season, along with nutrition-packed tropical fruits such as bananas, grapefruits, mangoes, oranges, pineapples, and pomegranates

- Keep most fruits at room temperature in baskets until ripe: apples, bananas, oranges, peaches, pears, pineapples, plums, and so on. Eat them or cook with them when they reach peak ripeness.
- Keep berries, grapes, and lemons in the refrigerator.

FROZEN BERRIES

- Keep in the freezer for up to 1 year.

SOFT DATES

- Keep in the refrigerator for up to 3 months.

DRIED FRUITS

Unsulfured only: apples, apricots, coconut, currants, dates, figs, prunes, and raisins

- Keep in labeled jars in a cupboard for up to 1 year.

Vegetables

MOST FRESH VEGETABLES IN SEASON

Beets, bell peppers, broccoli, cabbage, carrots, celery, leeks, lettuce and other greens, parsnips, radishes, rutabagas, turnips, yams, zucchini and other summer squash, and so on

- Keep in the refrigerator.

AVOCADOS

- Keep at room temperature until ripe. Once avocados are ripe, transfer to the refrigerator and keep for up to 3 days.

FRESH HERBS

Basil, cilantro, parsley, thyme, and so on

- Keep in the refrigerator for up to 1 week.

POTATOES, ONIONS, AND GARLIC

- Keep at room temperature in a cupboard, being sure potatoes aren't exposed to light. (Light will cause potatoes to turn green and sprout.)

TOMATOES

- Keep in a fruit basket until ripe.

FROZEN VEGETABLES

Corn, peas, and so on

- Keep in the freezer for up to 1 year.

Legumes and Legume Products

DRIED LEGUMES

Black beans, chickpeas, kidney beans, lentils, navy beans, pinto beans, split peas, and so on

- Keep in labeled jars in a cupboard for up to 1 year.

CANNED BEANS

- Keep in a cupboard for up to 2 years.

TOFU AND TEMPEH

- Keep in the refrigerator for up to 1 week or in the freezer for up to 3 months, but note that tofu that's been frozen will have a grainier texture.

Nuts and Seeds and Their Butters

NUTS

Raw almonds, Brazil nuts, cashews, pecans, walnuts, and so on

- Keep in labeled jars in a cupboard for up to 3 months or in the freezer for up to 1 year.

SEEDS FOR EATING

Chia, flax, hemp, pumpkin, sesame, and sunflower seeds

- Keep in labeled jars in a cupboard for up to 3 months or in the freezer for up to 1 year.

SEEDS FOR SPROUTING

Alfalfa, broccoli, buckwheat, clover, radish, and so on

- Keep in labeled jars in a cupboard for up to 2 years.

NUT AND SEED BUTTERS

Almond butter, peanut butter, tahini, and so on

- Stir to mix in any separated oil, then keep in the refrigerator for up to 3 months.

Oils

MOST OILS

Such as cold-pressed, expeller-pressed, or extra-virgin coconut, olive, sesame, and sunflower oil

- Keep in the refrigerator for up to 1 year. (Small jars of coconut, olive and sesame oil can be kept at room temperature to be used within 1 month.)

FLAXSEED OIL AND HEMPSEED OIL

- Keep in the refrigerator for up to 3 months.

Seasonings and Condiments

DRIED HERBS AND SPICES

Basil, cayenne, chili powder, cinnamon, coriander, cumin, curry powder, dill weed, oregano, paprika, rosemary, sage, tarragon, thyme, turmeric, and so on

- Keep in labeled jars in a cupboard for up to 2 years.

MOST OTHER SEASONINGS

Balsamic vinegar, cider vinegar, pepper, salt, tamari, and vegetable broth powder

- Keep in a cupboard for up to 2 years.

MISO AND OPEN CONTAINERS OF CONDIMENTS

Chili sauce, ketchup, vegan mayonnaise, mustard, pickle relish, and so on

- Keep in the refrigerator for up to 1 year, but note that some, such as vegan mayonnaise, should be used within a couple of months.

Sweeteners

MOST ALTERNATIVE SWEETENERS

Brown rice syrup, molasses, unrefined cane sugar, and so on

- Keep in a cupboard for up to 2 years.

MAPLE SYRUP

- Keep in the refrigerator for up to 1 year.

Miscellaneous

BREADS

Whole-grain, sprouted-grain, or gluten-free bread, tortillas, wraps, and so on

- Keep in the refrigerator for up to 1 week or in the freezer for up to 3 months.

NONDAIRY MILKS

Almond milk, help milk, rice milk, and so on

- Keep unopened containers in a cupboard for up to 1 year. Keep open containers in the refrigerator for up to 1 week.

WHOLE GRAINS AND WHOLE-GRAIN PRODUCTS

Baked corn chips, breakfast cereals, crackers, pastas, popcorn, rice cakes, whole-grain flours, whole grains, and so on

- Keep in containers or labeled jars in a cupboard for up to 1 year.

ASSORTED PANTRY STAPLES

Nutritional yeast, sea vegetables, vanilla and other extracts, and dry goods such as arrowroot powder, baking powder, and baking soda

- Keep in labeled jars in a cupboard for up to 2 years.

Three Weeks of Quick Dinners

You can make wholesome meals from scratch without spending hours in the kitchen. This section outlines five nights of weeknight dinners that should take less than thirty minutes to prepare. However, you may need to think ahead and soak or cook grains earlier in the day. Soups can be made in the morning or the previous evening and may need to simmer for a while. As you'll see, this meal plan is designed for diversity, featuring several ethnic cuisines and a variety of spices and flavorings throughout the week. Grains and starches vary from day to day. In general, each meal incorporates a legume. This includes tofu and tempeh, but with these soy products limited to once or twice per week. Also note that every meal includes some raw foods, which are such an important part of a healthful whole-foods diet.

Week 1

1. Greek Pasta Salad (page 106) and any steamed seasonal vegetable
2. Asian Quinoa and Tofu Salad (page 109)
3. Cauliflower, Spinach, and Potatoes in Mild Coconut Curry (page 146) and Carrot-Beet Salad (page 97)
4. Mediterranean Chickpea Soup (page 89), Cabbage Salad with Apple, Pecans, and Raisins (page 101), and Good Greens (page 154).
5. Pasta with Beans and Greens (page 140) and Sumptuous Caesar Salad (page 95)

Week 2

1. Baked Mixed Vegetables (page 158), Baked Tofu Fingers (page 156), and a green salad with Lemon Vinaigrette (page 117)
2. Cheesy Vegetable Pie (page 136) and raw vegetable sticks
3. Roasted New Potatoes with Tarragon Vinaigrette (page 161), Creamy Zucchini Soup (page 81), and a salad with Greek Salad Dressing (page 121)
4. Taco Salad with Chili (page 143)
5. Warming Vegetable Stew (page 124) and Carrot-Apple-Orange Juice (page 62)

Week 3

1. Curried Tofu with Apricots (page 152) and Kale-Avocado Salad (page 99)
2. Rice and Bean Salad with Cashews (page 110), green salad with Simple Oil and Vinegar Dressing (page 116), and any steamed seasonal vegetable
3. Vegetable Calzones (page 141) and Fresh Green Juice (page 63)
4. Heavenly Hummus (page 70) with raw vegetable sticks and Cashew Corn Chowder (page 82)
5. Vegan Macaroni and Cheese with Broccoli (page 138) and Winter Salad with Figs and Nuts (page 96)

APPENDIX F
Celebratory Menus

Celebratory occasions call for special meals. If you're transitioning to a whole-foods diet, you may wonder how to put together a meal that will enhance the occasion. Here are a few suggestions. Once you're familiar with whole-foods recipes and have developed a repertoire of favorites, you'll undoubtedly develop menus that you and your family will cherish for years to come.

FALL AND WINTER MEAL FOR SPECIAL OCCASIONS

- Almond-Mushroom Pâté (page 74) on whole-grain crackers
- Cashew-Carrot Loaf (page 133) with Creamy Tamari Gravy (page 113)
- Root Fries (page 160)
- Winter Salad with Figs and Nuts (page 96)
- Steamed Brussels sprouts seasoned with freshly squeezed lemon juice

SPRING AND SUMMER MEAL FOR SPECIAL OCCASIONS

- Veggie Pâté (page 76) on raw sweet potato slices
- Curried Tofu with Apricots (page 152) or Marinated Vegetable and Tofu Kabobs (page 130) served on cooked quinoa
- Summer Salad with Herbs and Garden Vegetables (page 94)
- Beets and Greens with Lemon-Basil Dressing (page 102)
- Fresh corn on the cob

HOLIDAY WHOLE-FOODS MEAL

- Creamy Spinach-Basil Spread (page 68) on whole-grain crackers
- Curried Winter Squash Soup (page 83)
- Eggplant-Pecan Patties (page 131) with Creamy Tamari Gravy (page 113)
- Baked Sweet Potatoes with Rosemary and Maple Syrup (page 157)
- Fresh Cranberry Relish (page 112)
- Sweet Kale Salad (page 100)
- Steamed beets, seasoned with balsamic vinegar

BRUNCH

- Creamy Fruit Shake (page 56)
- Scrambled Tofu (page 46)
- Vegan French Toast (page 45)
- Roasted New Potatoes with Tarragon Vinaigrette (page 161)
- Cabbage Salad with Apple, Pecans, and Raisins (page 101)
- Pear-Ginger Muffins (page 49)

About the Author

Caroline Marie Dupont, MSc, has been exploring, living, and teaching an integrated approach to health for over twenty years. She is the author of the book and DVD *Enlightened Eating*, several meditation CDs, and the *ClearBeing Holistic Home Fitness Program* DVD. Caroline is a senior instructor at the Canadian School of Natural Nutrition, and because she believes that nutrition is best learned in kitchens and gardens, she has taught hundreds of food-preparation classes to thousands of students. Caroline also leads meditation classes and offers private consultations, various courses, and Deep Healing Retreats. For more information, visit carolinedupont.com.

Index

Page references in *italics* refer to illustrations or sidebars. Recipe titles appear in *italics*.

W

walnuts, in recipes, 42, 98

Warming Vegetable Stew, 124–25

water

    guidelines for drinking, 17, 22, *36, 37*

    in layering of food, 22

watermelon, in fruit drink, 55

weight imbalances, toxins and, *26*

wheat, 2, 10

White Bean Dip, Creamy, 71

white flour, as antinutrient/toxin, 15, 25

whole foods/whole-foods diet, 2, 12–13, 29

Wild Greens Smoothie, 60

Wild Rice and Fiddlehead Salad, 104

Winter Salad with Figs and Nuts, 96

Winter Squash Soup, Curried, 83

wraps, for packed lunches, 35

Y

yams, 76

Z

Zesty Bean Chili, 88

Zucchini Soup, Creamy, 81

BOOK PUBLISHING Co.

books that educate, inspire, and empower

To find your favorite vegetarian and soyfood products online, visit:
healthy-eating.com

Cooking Vegan

Vesanto Melina, MS, RD,
Joseph Forest

978-1-57067-267-5

$19.95

Enlightened Eating (DVD)

Caroline Marie Dupont

978-157067-256-9

$19.95

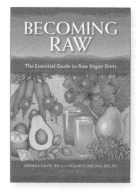

Becoming Raw

Brenda Davis, RD,
Vesanto Melina, MS, RD,
with Rynn Berry

978-1-57067-238-5

$24.95

Natural Vegan Kitchen

Christine Waltermyer

978-1-57067-245-3

$19.95

The Allergy-Free Cook Bakes Bread

Laurie Sadowski

978-1-57067-262-0

$14.95

Jazzy Vegetarian

Laura Theodore

978-1-57067-261-3

$24.95

Purchase these health titles and cookbooks from your local bookstore or natural food store,
or you can buy them directly from:

Book Publishing Company • P.O. Box 99 • Summertown, TN 38483 • 1-800-695-2241

Please include $3.95 per book for shipping and handling.